jB
B18s

MAR - 2004

JOSEPHINE BAKER

JOSEPHINE BAKER

Alan Schroeder

Senior Consulting Editor
Nathan Irvin Huggins
Director
W.E.B. Du Bois Institute for Afro-American Research
Harvard University

CHELSEA HOUSE PUBLISHERS
Philadelphia

Chelsea House Publishers
Editor-in-Chief   Remmel Nunn
Managing Editor   Karyn Gullen Browne
Copy Chief   Juliann Barbato
Picture Editor   Adrian G. Allen
Art Director   Maria Epes
Deputy Copy Chief   Mark Rifkin
Assistant Art Director   Noreen Romano
Manufacturing Manager   Gerald Levine
Systems Manager   Lindsey Ottman
Production Manager   Joseph Romano
Production Coordinator   Marie Claire Cebrián

Black Americans of Achievement
Senior Editor   Richard Rennert

Staff for JOSEPHINE BAKER
Copy Editor   Brian Sookram
Editorial Assistant   Michele Haddad
Picture Researcher   Patricia Burns
Designer   Ghila Krajzman
Cover Illustration   Bernie Fuchs, from a photograph by George
Hoyningen-Huene, Courtesy Horst Studio

*To my good friends in St. Louis, Elizabeth Merritt
and Richard Martin, Jr.*   —A. S.

7   9   8

Library of Congress Cataloging-in-Publication Data
Schroeder, Alan.
    Josephine Baker/by Alan Schroeder.
        p.   cm.—(Black Americans of achievement)
    Includes bibliographical references (p.) and index.
    Summary: Biography of the black American singer and dancer who
achieved fame in Paris in the 1920s and was awarded the French
Legion of Honor for her work during World War II.
    ISBN 0-7910-1116-X
          0-7910-1142-9 (pbk.)
    1. Baker, Josephine, 1906–75—Juvenile literature.   2. Dancers—
France—Biography—Juvenile literature.   3. Afro-American
entertainers—France—Biography—Juvenile literature.
[1. Baker, Josephine, 1906–75. 2. Dancers. 3. Afro-Americans—
Biography.]
I. Title.   II. Series.
GV1785.B3S37   1991
792.8′092—dc20   90-2537
[B]   CIP
[92]   AC

Frontispiece: *Josephine Baker
performs a humorous number at
the Folies-Bergère in 1927. Later
in the show, she cut a more
elegant figure, wearing red gloves
with diamond balls hanging from
the tips of her fingers.*

CONTENTS

BLACK AMERICANS OF ACHIEVEMENT

HENRY AARON
baseball great

KAREEM ABDUL-JABBAR
basketball great

MUHAMMAD ALI
heavyweight champion

RICHARD ALLEN
religious leader and social activist

MAYA ANGELOU
author

LOUIS ARMSTRONG
musician

ARTHUR ASHE
tennis great

JOSEPHINE BAKER
entertainer

JAMES BALDWIN
author

TYRA BANKS
model

BENJAMIN BANNEKER
scientist and mathematician

AMIRI BARAKA
poet and playwright

COUNT BASIE
bandleader and composer

ROMARE BEARDEN
artist

JAMES BECKWOURTH
frontiersman

MARY McLEOD BETHUNE
educator

GEORGE WASHINGTON CARVER
botanist

CHARLES CHESNUTT
author

JOHNNIE COCHRAN
lawyer

BILL COSBY
entertainer

PAUL CUFFE
merchant and abolitionist

MILES DAVIS
musician

FATHER DIVINE
religious leader

FREDERICK DOUGLASS
abolitionist editor

CHARLES DREW
physician

W. E. B. DU BOIS
scholar and activist

PAUL LAURENCE DUNBAR
poet

DUKE ELLINGTON
bandleader and composer

RALPH ELLISON
author

JULIUS ERVING
basketball great

LOUIS FARRAKHAN
political activist

ELLA FITZGERALD
singer

MORGAN FREEMAN
actor

MARCUS GARVEY
black nationalist leader

JOSH GIBSON
baseball great

WHOOPI GOLDBERG
entertainer

CUBA GOODING JR.
actor

ALEX HALEY
author

PRINCE HALL
social reformer

JIMI HENDRIX
musician

MATTHEW HENSON
explorer

GREGORY HINES
performer

BILLIE HOLIDAY
singer

LENA HORNE
entertainer

WHITNEY HOUSTON
singer and actress

LANGSTON HUGHES
poet

ZORA NEALE HURSTON
author

JANET JACKSON
musician

JESSE JACKSON
civil-rights leader and politician

MICHAEL JACKSON
entertainer

SAMUEL L. JACKSON
actor

T. D. JAKES
religious leader

JACK JOHNSON
heavyweight champion

MAGIC JOHNSON
basketball great

SCOTT JOPLIN
composer

BARBARA JORDAN
politician

MICHAEL JORDAN
basketball great

CORETTA SCOTT KING
civil-rights leader

MARTIN LUTHER KING, JR.
civil-rights leader

LEWIS LATIMER
scientist

SPIKE LEE
filmmaker

CARL LEWIS
champion athlete

JOE LOUIS
heavyweight champion

RONALD McNAIR
astronaut

MALCOLM X
militant black leader

BOB MARLEY
musician

THURGOOD MARSHALL
Supreme Court justice

TONI MORRISON
author

ELIJAH MUHAMMAD
religious leader

EDDIE MURPHY
entertainer

JESSE OWENS
champion athlete

SATCHEL PAIGE
baseball great

CHARLIE PARKER
musician

ROSA PARKS
civil-rights leader

COLIN POWELL
military leader

PAUL ROBESON
singer and actor

JACKIE ROBINSON
baseball great

CHRIS ROCK
comedian/actor

DIANA ROSS
entertainer

WILL SMITH
actor

CLARENCE THOMAS
Supreme Court justice

SOJOURNER TRUTH
antislavery activist

HARRIET TUBMAN
antislavery activist

NAT TURNER
slave revolt leader

TINA TURNER
entertainer

DENMARK VESEY
slave revolt leader

ALICE WALKER
author

MADAM C. J. WALKER
entrepreneur

BOOKER T. WASHINGTON
educator

DENZEL WASHINGTON
actor

J. C. WATTS
politician

VANESSA WILLIAMS
singer and actress

OPRAH WINFREY
entertainer

TIGER WOODS
golf star

RICHARD WRIGHT
author

ON ACHIEVEMENT

Coretta Scott King

BEFORE YOU BEGIN this book, I hope you will ask yourself what the word excellence means to you. I think that it's a question we should all ask, and keep asking as we grow older and change. Because the truest answer to it should never change. When you think of excellence, perhaps you think of success at work; or of becoming wealthy; or meeting the right person, getting married, and having a good family life.

Those important goals are worth striving for, but there is a better way to look at excellence. As Martin Luther King, Jr., said in one of his last sermons, "I want you to be first in love. I want you to be first in moral excellence. I want you to be first in generosity. If you want to be important, wonderful. If you want to be great, wonderful. But recognize that he who is greatest among you shall be your servant."

My husband, Martin Luther King, Jr., knew that the true meaning of achievement is service. When I met him, in 1952, he was already ordained as a Baptist preacher and was working towards a doctoral degree at Boston University. I was studying at the New England Conservatory and dreamed of accomplishments in music. We married a year later, and after I graduated the following year we moved to Montgomery, Alabama. We didn't know it then, but our notions of achievement were about to undergo a dramatic change.

You may have read or heard about what happened next. What began with the boycott of a local bus line grew into a national movement, and by the time he was assassinated in 1968 my husband had fashioned a black movement powerful enough to shatter forever the practice of racial segregation. What you may not have read about is where he got his method for resisting injustice without compromising his religious beliefs.

He adopted the strategy of nonviolence from a man of a different race, who lived in a distant country, and even practiced a different religion. The man was Mahatma Gandhi, the great leader of India, who devoted his life to serving humanity in the spirit of love and nonviolence. It was in these principles that Martin discovered his method for social reform. More than anything else, those two principles were the key to his achievements.

This book is about black Americans who served society through the excellence of their achievements. It forms a part of the rich history of black men and women in America—a history of stunning accomplishments in every field of human endeavor, from literature and art to science, industry, education, diplomacy, athletics, jurisprudence, even polar exploration.

Not all of the people in this history had the same ideals, but I think you will find something that all of them have in common. Like Martin Luther King, Jr., they all decided to become "drum majors" and serve humanity. In that principle—whether it was expressed in books, inventions, or song—they found something outside themselves to use as a goal and a guide. Something that showed them a way to serve others, instead of living only for themselves.

Reading the stories of these courageous men and women not only helps us discover the principles that we will use to guide our own lives but also teaches us about our black heritage and about America itself. It is crucial for us to know the heroes and heroines of our history and to realize that the price we paid in our struggle for equality in America was dear. But we must also understand that we have gotten as far as we have partly because America's democratic system and ideals made it possible.

We are still struggling with racism and prejudice. But the great men and women in this series are a tribute to the spirit of our democratic ideals and the system in which they have flourished. And that makes their stories special and worth knowing. ❧

JOSEPHINE BAKER

1

"IF AN ORCHID COULD SIZZLE . . ."

JOSEPHINE BAKER WAS just 19 years old when she made her first appearance on the stage of the Folies-Bergère. The Parisian theater, she later wrote, "had a fountain, a canopy as a sky and chandeliers to provide the sunlight." The oldest and most spectacular music hall in the world, the Folies-Bergère was an appropriate showcase for the sensationally talented Josephine Baker.

In April 1926, when Baker debuted in *La Folie du Jour*, the Parisian music halls were at the height of their creativity. Nothing could rival them for sheer, eye-popping spectacle. Like the Hollywood movie studios of the 1930s, the Folies-Bergère resembled a large and efficient entertainment factory. The finished product, as the director liked to say, was "three enchanting hours of fantasy and beauty and fun, an evening's escape into the land of dream-fulfillment."

During this splashy postwar period, it was not unusual for a Folies production to cost half a million dollars. Most Parisians agreed, however, that it was money well spent—especially in 1926, when Josephine Baker starred in *La Folie du Jour*.

Her opening-night appearance in that show has gone down as one of *the* great moments in music hall history. The curtain rose to reveal a steamy jungle

One of the world's most flamboyant and best-loved entertainers, Baker was like a freshly uncorked bottle of champagne, bubbling and exotic. "If an orchid could sizzle," wrote the Los Angeles Examiner, *"it would be something like Josephine Baker."*

11

setting: kapok trees, a winding river, birdcalls, heavy swinging vines. Native drumbeats could be heard in the distance. Then, high above the stage, Baker made her entrance, crawling backward, catlike, down one of the painted trees. She was not bedecked in a feathered headdress, like most Folies stars. Springing to the stage, landing on all fours like a panther, Baker was wearing nothing but a skirt of brilliant yellow bananas.

The costume was so striking, so fabulously primitive, the Parisians leaped to their feet, crying out in surprise. The conductor slashed the air with his baton, and with the shouts and the applause ringing in her ears, Baker began dancing, the bananas jumping violently with every choreographed move. It was five minutes of sheer theatrical genius.

An hour later, Baker returned and, wearing a grass skirt, she performed the Charleston on a polished mirror, her knees twisting in and out in a dizzying blur. But it was the banana dance that fascinated everyone. When it was over, Baker threw up her arms and, with a breathtaking leap, landed on top of an artificial palm tree. Panting, she grinned and rolled her eyes at the audience.

The applause was shattering. The Parisians had never witnessed anything like it—certainly never at the Folies-Bergère. They rushed into the aisles as the curtain came ringing down.

"Encore! Encore!"

The shouting reached a frenzy, and Baker was forced to return. With a beautiful blue spotlight fixed upon her, she took 12 curtain calls. The young American from St. Louis, Missouri, had been onstage for only a few minutes, but she had won for herself a lifetime of fame and admiration.

Wherever Josephine Baker went now, photographers hurried after her. Reporters scribbled down her every comment. Fashion designers delivered arm-

A playful Baker poses in the celebrated banana skirt she wore at the Folies-Bergère in 1926.

loads of beautiful dresses to her apartment on the rue Beaujon. Josephine Baker dolls appeared on the streets of Paris, each wearing a little skirt of bananas. In one fell swoop, she had become the most famous woman in the city, surpassing Mistinguett, who until that night had been the queen of the French music halls.

Young Parisiennes began copying Baker's closely cut hair, which, from a distance, looked as though it had been tarred to her head.

"Are you a boy or a girl?" people frequently asked. Baker just smiled.

Baker at the height of her career, in her dressing room at the Casino de Paris music hall. "Since I personified the savage on the stage," she said, "I tried to be as civilized as possible in daily life."

The chocolate color of her skin became all the rage, and thousands of women smeared themselves with walnut oil and sunbathed for hours to look like the Black Pearl of the Folies-Bergère.

Night after night, different men took Baker out on the town, showering her with expensive gifts: pearls, diamonds, 14-carat–gold fingernail polish, imported flower baskets, rings, bracelets, perfumes. On her 20th birthday, one admirer presented her with a new Voisin car.

"She is all but the dictator of Paris," one magazine wrote. Famed artist Pablo Picasso, for whom Baker posed, had a different way of putting it. He likened her to the most glamorous queen of ancient Egypt, saying, "She is the Nefertiti of now."

In the late 1920s, Baker rivaled movie stars Gloria Swanson and Mary Pickford as the most photographed woman in the world. She was painted, sketched, caricatured, and filmed. All told, more than a dozen books have been written about her.

It seems remarkable, then, that the average American knows very little about Josephine Baker. She enjoyed one of the most flamboyant and, at the same time, one of the most controversial careers in show business. She was also one of the first crusaders for black civil rights; as early as the 1940s, she was forcing people to acknowledge the unfairness of racial discrimination. Sadly, Baker's dream of international brotherhood did not reflect the dreams of postwar American society.

Though she considered France her spiritual home, Josephine Baker never forgot her roots, and she returned to America several times to renew them. These visits, spread out over a number of years, were not always easy. Yet they strengthened her tremendously, not only as an entertainer but as a black woman who valued her dignity and knew when to fight for it. ❧

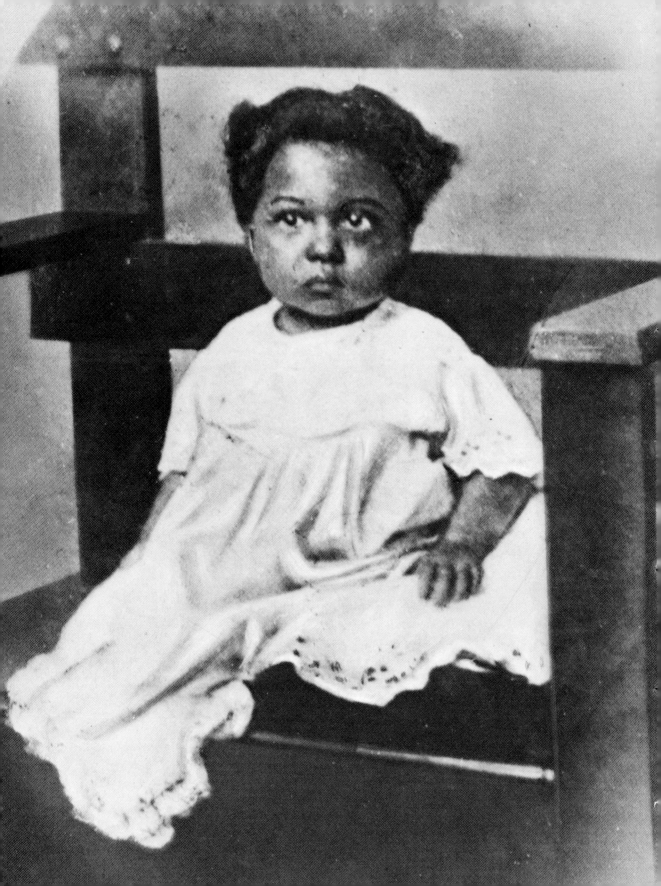

2

TUMPIE

J OSEPHINE BAKER WAS born on June 3, 1906, in St. Louis, Missouri, and it was there that she spent her earliest years. A heavy baby, she was nicknamed Tumpie, an accidental variation on Humpty Dumpty. ("Mama," she admitted years later, "hadn't heard the poem quite right.")

Josephine's mother, Carrie McDonald, was a washerwoman who had arrived in the riverside city in 1904 seeking a better life for herself. She was able to find work quickly, taking in laundry and keeping house for well-to-do white families. A hard worker, Carrie also had dreams of becoming an entertainer, and it was in a local production of a play that she met Eddie Carson, who fathered Josephine.

Eddie Carson was a honky-tonk drummer, a fun-loving fellow who performed in the smoky bar-relhouses and gambling halls that made up the notorious section of town called Chestnut Valley. Like most musicians, Eddie played because he felt he had to. Music was his life, his joy, and in the early 1900s there was no better place for a honky-tonk drummer to find work than St. Louis. Musically, it was one of the most important cities in the nation, attracting many gifted ragtime composers. It was

The future entertainer at age two. Baker inherited her love of the theater from her parents, who performed song-and-dance routines in vaudeville houses in St. Louis, Missouri.

17

there, on the banks of the Mississippi, that Scott Joplin wrote his earliest piano music before going to Chicago to pursue his career.

Several nights a week, Carrie took Josephine to the crowded gambling halls and dimly lit honky-tonks to hear Eddie and his friends play. These jazzmen were performing the most exciting music in the country, and many of Josephine's earliest memories were of the sounds, and not the sights, of St. Louis.

Not long after Josephine's birth, Carrie had another baby, a boy named Richard. Eddie, meanwhile, began spending more and more time away from home. He was not ready for the demands of fatherhood, demands that might take him away from the music he loved. In time, he packed his things and moved out.

Carrie was bitterly disappointed by Eddie's departure. She was a strong, practical woman, however, and realizing that she had two small children to feed, she married a factory worker named Arthur Martin, a moody fellow who felt that life had never given him a fair shake. Because Arthur had a quick temper, which made it difficult for him to hold down a job for any length of time, Carrie was forced to take in laundry to pay the bills. Life, it often seemed, was nothing but one long struggle to pay the rent (or figure out a way not to pay it). The family was always moving, always trying to stay one step ahead of the landlord.

In time, Carrie had two more daughters, Margaret and Willie Mae. To make things easier for the family, Josephine was frequently sent to live with Grandma McDonald, a warm, loving woman who liked to bake cookies and read bedtime stories to her granddaughter. These stories, fairy tales mostly, filled Josephine's head with visions of princes and castles and white horses and beautiful women. They helped her escape, at least for a little while, the hardships of home.

One Sunday, while returning from church, Josephine stepped on a rusty nail, which pierced her foot. By the time she got home, her leg was swollen from blood poisoning. Carrie rushed her to the doctor, who recommended that the leg be cut off. Josephine took one look at the amputation saw and became hysterical.

To calm her down, the doctor slowly drained the wound. Josephine nearly fainted when she saw that her blood had turned black. Fortunately, her leg did not need to be amputated, although it was nearly a month before she could walk normally. The doctor's bill became yet another burden for the family to bear.

Each morning, Arthur walked to one of the factories in St. Louis and waited at the gate to see if there was any work that day. Landing a job was largely a matter of being in the right place at the right time, and Arthur rarely was. Usually, he came home with nothing more than a sour look on his face. While Carrie prepared dinner, he would complain bitterly about society, about how difficult it was for a black man to get ahead in St. Louis.

Many evenings, after their meal, Arthur would tell Josephine and the other children about a dream he had. He believed that the day would come when all people would be free—free of prejudice, free of hate—and on that glorious day, blacks and whites would live together in harmony. Trust would be their common bond. It was a hope that Arthur cherished. Like Carrie's deep belief in God, it somehow made the burden of life seem a little lighter.

In addition to Arthur's dreams and Grandma McDonald's fairy tales, there was always music to comfort Josephine. The whole city of St. Louis was alive with it. Music could be heard in the cafés and wine rooms in the afternoons, and it heated up the honky-tonks every night. Long after the sun had gone down, Josephine would lie in bed and listen to the lively sounds of ragtime, as well as a sadder, more haunting kind of music: the blues.

Josephine's parents had performed together in the city's vaudeville houses, and it was only natural that Josephine took an interest in performing, too. She began dancing for a practical reason: to keep herself warm during the cold Missouri winters. When spring came, however, she continued to dance because it made her happy, and like the fairy tales, it helped her forget the family's troubles.

Every now and then, when she could afford it, Josephine went to the Booker T. Washington Theater, a black vaudeville house at 23rd and Market. Famous black entertainers such as Ma Rainey and Bessie Smith performed there frequently, and in the darkness of that small theater Josephine could lose herself in a world of bright lights and pretty costumes and wonderful music. She especially liked watching the chorus girls as they sashayed their way across the stage, legs kicking, feathers flying. Listening to peppy songs such as "Bake That Chicken Pie" and "Razzazza Mazzazza," Josephine must have wished that she too could be up there performing.

To amuse themselves, the neighborhood children began staging their own vaudeville shows, copying whatever was playing that week at the Booker T. Admission was a penny, and Josephine usually made up one-half of the two-girl chorus line. It was during these simple productions that Josephine began to think that someday she might like to become a dancer. Maybe she would perform on the stage of the Booker T. Washington Theater, maybe even meet Bessie Smith, the Queen of the Blues. . . .

As Josephine grew older, however, she discovered she had less and less time to dream. As the eldest child, she had to begin pulling her own weight.

Known as Queen of the Blues, Bessie Smith sang often at the Booker T. Washington Theater, a black vaudeville house in St. Louis that Baker visited whenever she could afford it.

Schooling was all right, Carrie felt, but it was more important for a young black girl to learn household chores, which would enable her to earn a living. And so Josephine was sent to live with a Mrs. Keiser, who gave the child room and board in exchange for household work.

As it turned out, the arrangement was not a fair one. Keiser was a cruel woman who worked Josephine constantly, beating her with a stick until blisters appeared on her back. The evening meals were never plentiful, and Josephine's bed was nothing more than a wooden box in the cellar, which she had to share with a crippled dog named Three Legs.

This unhappy arrangement came to an end when Josephine accidentally cracked some dinner plates. Keiser, in a fit of anger, seized Josephine's arm and plunged it into a pot of boiling water. The pain was so great that Josephine fainted. When she awoke, she found herself in a hospital.

As soon as she was well, however, it was necessary for Josephine to look for another job. In the winter, she earned a few coins by going from house to house and shoveling snow; in the summer, she rang door-bells and offered to baby-sit or scrub floors. She gave what little money she made to Carrie, usually keeping a nickel for herself. Five nickels, after all, was enough to get into the Booker T. Washington Theater.

Marcus Avenue, a typical East St. Louis street, as it appeared during Baker's youth. She was eager to move away from the city after its black ghetto was attacked by white mobs in the July 1917 riot.

By this time, Josephine's family was living in a one-room shack in Boxcar Town, in East St. Louis. It was a dirty, depressing neighborhood. True to its name, many of the "houses" were nothing more than abandoned boxcars.

Arthur did his best to make the shack livable by hanging scraps of newspaper on the wall for wallpaper. Realizing how much it meant to Josephine, Carrie allowed her to raise two puppies, whom she fed old pieces of bread dipped in Sunday's milk. But these small gestures barely helped to make life in Boxcar Town more agreeable.

Rats, the family discovered, were a constant menace, and flattened tin cans were hammered over the holes in the floor to keep them out. This tactic rarely worked: The rats gnawed through the metal. Terrified, Josephine would watch as her brother, Richard, sat up in bed and picked them off with a slingshot.

Sometimes, there was not enough money to buy food, and Josephine spent many afternoons searching through the trash for a fish head or spoiled potato to put into her mother's soup. At times, it seemed like life could not get any harder.

Then, one evening in July 1917, tragedy struck. Josephine was asleep in bed when she suddenly felt her patchwork quilt being yanked back. Before she could understand what was happening, Carrie had pulled her to her feet, begging her to get dressed as quickly as she could. It was a frightening moment, full of confusion and panic. As Arthur lit a lantern, Josephine watched her mother tear through the bureau drawers, frantically grabbing what little money the family had.

Carrie had good reason to be afraid. Half an hour earlier, East St. Louis had exploded in a racial riot. Increasing numbers of southern blacks, in search of work, had been moving north to St. Louis for more than a decade. Many of them landed jobs at the local factories because they did not need to be paid as much as white workers. The lower-class whites bitterly resented this situation and wanted to change it; labor agitators intensified the problem by spreading lurid rumors of atrocious crimes committed by blacks.

Finally, on the night of July 2, the frustrated white workers decided to take matters into their own hands. Open warfare—extermination of the black troublemakers—seemed the only answer. Grabbing whatever weapons they could find, they stormed across the Eads Bridge toward Boxcar Town.

Warnings sped through the back alleys, but for many it was too late. By the time Carrie managed to push her family outdoors, the sky was already red

with flames, and the night air was filled with screaming as blacks were hunted down and clubbed in the
streets. Fences were trampled, windows were shattered, and boxcars exploded in violent flames.

Clutching her two puppies to her chest, Josephine felt herself pushed to the ground. Carrie
covered her children as best she could, while dozens
of terrified families ran through the streets, dragging
their few possessions behind them in broken-down
baby carriages. A few feet from where Carrie was
crouching, a black man was knocked to the ground;
a moment later, a white man began beating him
savagely with a club. It was a horrifying and bloody
scene, one that Josephine would never forget. In
later years, she always referred to the East St. Louis
riot as the worst memory of her childhood.

After several hours, the melee finally came to an
end. The flames in the boxcars died, having nothing
left to feed upon. Emergency first-aid and shelter
stations were set up, and with the arrival of dawn,
the now-homeless black community returned to sal-
vage what it could from the smoking debris. In all, 39
blacks and 9 whites had been murdered. Property
damage exceeded half a million dollars.

The riot, understandably, was a turning point in
Josephine's life. As she walked past the long lines of
people waiting for Red Cross handouts, she realized,
perhaps for the first time, that she would have to be
strong, very strong, to survive in a white man's
world. According to Josephine, she made a vow that
day that when she became an adult, she would try to
make it easier for blacks and whites to get along.

At that moment, however, Arthur's dream of
universal brotherhood must have seemed nearly impossible. ❧

3

ON THE ROAD

THE EAST ST. Louis riot of 1917 devastated the black community, and it was some time before Carrie Martin could get her family back on its feet. With her husband Arthur still unemployed, she began taking in more laundry than ever, and she put Josephine to work scrubbing trousers and petticoats in the sink. The hours were long and the work was backbreaking, and Josephine hated every minute of it. She saw washing as a dead-end life.

Desperate to escape the piles of laundry, Josephine became a waitress at the Old Chauffeur's Club on Pine Street. It was not easy work, but it was a lot more enjoyable than scrubbing, and besides, the Old Chauffeur's Club was right next door to Pythian Hall, where Eddie Carson's band was playing. Eddie enjoyed the hours he spent with his daughter, and Josephine loved listening to the band.

It was during this time that Josephine did an unexpected thing, one that surprised not only Carrie but the entire family: She got married.

Like many black men in St. Louis, Willie Wells worked in a foundry. Josephine probably met him at one of the neighborhood dances. Only 13 at the time, she knew little about life and even less about men. The marriage was probably a whim of the moment, or simply a frustrated attempt by Josephine

Baker was a born comedienne who spent most of her early stage career playing humorous roles. But in 1924, when she made her Broadway debut in The Chocolate Dandies, *she was allowed to forgo her usual costume, which included blackface makeup and clown shoes; for the first time, the public saw her glamorous side.*

to escape her life at home. Either way, the marriage was short-lived, ending one night when the newly-weds got into a violent fight. Josephine broke a bottle to defend herself, and Willie stormed out of the house, never to reappear.

Confused and unhappy, Josephine returned to her waitressing job at the Old Chauffeur's Club. Now, she not only wanted to escape her life at home, she wanted to get out of St. Louis altogether. She sensed, perhaps correctly, that the city held little opportunity for her.

Josephine soon discovered a way out. In late 1919, she met a ragtag trio of performers called the Jones Family Band. Old Man Jones played a brass horn, his wife played the trumpet, and their pretty daughter, Doll, was a fiddler. During her breaks at the Old Chauffeur's Club, Josephine entertained the customers by singing songs and doing a few easy dance steps. Old Man Jones liked what he saw, and on the spur of the moment he invited her to join their trio. Josephine needed no time to think the matter over. On the spot, she quit her job and joined the Family Band.

Performing in cafés and restaurants and barbershops was exhausting, even embarrassing, and sometimes Josephine wondered if she had made the right decision. The Joneses did not pay her, although they at least taught her to play the trombone. Old Man Jones firmly believed that a person could never have too many talents.

The hard work eventually paid off, however: The Jones Family Band was invited to play for a week at the Booker T. Washington Theater. Opening night was memorable. Josephine's costume was much too big for her, but instead of letting the long dress interfere with her dancing, she cleverly, and humorously, made it the visual focus of the act. Even at this early stage of her career, Josephine seemed to understand the fundamentals of theatrical comedy. Rolling her eyes outrageously, she was a natural comedienne, and the audience rewarded her nightly with gales of laughter.

The Dixie Steppers were the stars of the show, and both the Steppers and the Jones Family Band were asked to stay on for a second week. They did, and at the end of the engagement, another invitation came, this one even more unexpected: The Steppers asked the Jones Family Band to join them on their upcoming tour of the South.

Old Man Jones agreed to go, then asked Josephine if she would also be coming. After all, he explained, she was part of the Family now.

Josephine knew how important this moment was, and without thinking twice, she said yes. This was her one chance to escape St. Louis, to get away from the dirty dishes at the Old Chauffeur's Club and the piles of laundry in Carrie's apartment. She immediately hurried home, told her mother what had happened, threw her things into a beat-up suitcase, and was on the midnight train for Tennessee.

Years later, Josephine Baker remembered the satisfaction she felt as the locomotive pulled out of St. Louis's Union Station: "Closing my eyes, I dreamed of sunlit cities, magnificent theaters and me in the limelight. . . . Dizzy with delight and exhaustion," she said, she fell asleep, her head leaning against the Pullman car window, a half-eaten sandwich resting in her lap.

Life on the road, Josephine discovered, was entirely different from anything she had ever experienced before. It was exhilarating, it was exhausting, and it was also a little frightening. The discrimination that Josephine experienced in St. Louis intensified the farther south she traveled.

Dancing off the train, swinging their baggage and cracking vaudeville jokes, the Dixie Steppers and the

Jones Family Band were frequently met with cold, unfriendly stares. Porters refused to help them with their heavy trunks, and it was nearly impossible to find a room in a decent boardinghouse. Lunch counters, public rest rooms, streetcars, and water fountains were all strictly segregated. Josephine grew to hate the familiar cardboard sign For Whites Only.

Ethel Waters, a well-known blues singer, was also touring the southern circuit in 1920, and Sweet Mama Stringbean left a vivid account of this period in her autobiography, *His Eye Is On the Sparrow:* "The white people I encountered in the South never overlooked a chance to put me in my place. . . . If I went to buy something in an Atlanta store, the white clerk would give me one look and say: 'I see you're one of those fresh Yankee niggers.' . . . I [also] noticed that we of the stage were considered not much better than cattle by respectable Negroes."

In the years immediately following World War I, black entertainment had not yet come into its own. Bessie Smith, Ida Cox, and Ma Rainey all had loyal followings, but these singers were the exceptions. Negro vaudeville in 1920 was a rough-and-tumble affair. Most of the theaters Josephine encountered were cold, seedy firetraps, with dripping pipes, makeshift chairs, and scurrying cockroaches. Candles provided the only light, and the small pickup orchestra was usually out of tune. Now that she could see it for what it was, the world of black vaudeville was disappointing, but in Josephine's opinion, it was still a lot better than scrubbing dirty bloomers.

Whenever she was not performing onstage, Josephine was helping the Steppers with their props, or sewing costumes, or packing the trunks, or stirring up dishes of chow mein over a second-hand hot plate. Every day was different on the vaudeville circuit, and Josephine learned as much as she could as quickly as she could. She was like a sponge, picking up all the tricks of the trade.

Importantly, she learned how to get laughs. In her opening scene with the Jones Family Band, Josephine played a winged Cupid suspended from the rafters. During one performance, though, her pasteboard wings got caught on the curtain, and the harder she struggled to release herself, the harder the audience laughed. After a stagehand had carefully lowered her to safety, the manager came running up. Josephine, in tears, was certain she was going to be fired. Instead, the manager raved about her comic performance and insisted she do it the same way every night. Cupid's clumsy appearance became the highlight of the show.

By the time the troupe arrived in New Orleans, Josephine considered herself an experienced performer. The only thing she worried about was her body. A thin child, with bean pole legs and an average face, she wondered if she would ever be pretty enough to be a chorus girl. She toyed with the idea of appearing in whiteface, but Clara Smith, the star of the show, assured her that talent, and not skin color, was what mattered in show business. To fatten Josephine up, however, Clara began feeding her thick slices of sweet potato pie before each matinee.

Near the end of the New Orleans engagement, the Jones Family Band decided they had had enough of the vaudeville circuit. Old Man Jones announced that his family was quitting the business. Josephine was shocked.

A second bombshell dropped when the Dixie Steppers told Josephine that without the Family Band they had no place for her in their act. She was too light skinned, they said. She did not fit in with the rest of the chorus girls.

Josephine panicked. She desperately wanted to stay in vaudeville. So, at the end of the New Orleans engagement, she did a daring thing. As the Steppers prepared to move on to another town, she slipped into one of their unlocked shipping crates, which was

Composer Eubie Blake (left) and lyricist Noble Sissle wrote the sparkling score for Shuffle Along, *the all-black show that revolutionized the American theater. Baker toured with the main company for more than a year after Broadway's first black musical reached the end of its New York run.*

soon hoisted onto the train with the rest of the baggage. Three hours later, she emerged, half-frozen, the tips of her fingers blue from the cold.

The Dixie Steppers were highly annoyed, but they also admired Josephine's determination. Unsure as to how they would fit her into the act, they decided to hire her at nine dollars a week. She would be an "odds-and-ends girl," doing whatever needed to be done at the moment.

Now Josephine worked twice as hard, repairing costumes, polishing shoes, painting scenery, sewing buttons, passing out handbills on street corners. She would do anything, anything at all, just to get on the stage and make people laugh and applaud. She never fit in with the rest of the chorus, but the Steppers quickly realized that maybe that was not such a bad thing. Josephine had personality—people laughed when she walked onstage. In vaudeville, where so

Baker (first dancer on right) leads the Shuffle Along *chorus line. Although her ability to dance out of step and play the clown irked her fellow dancers, her comedic talents helped make her a box-office draw.*

much depended on visual humor, that was a rare gift. "I became the show's 'funny girl,'" Josephine remembered.

After touring the southern states, the Steppers turned north, eventually pulling into Philadelphia. There, Josephine met an easygoing young man named William Howard Baker. Willie, as she called him, was a Pullman porter, and the two hit it off immediately. Willie was impressed with her exciting life as an entertainer; she, in turn, admired his honest and gentle nature. As a vaudevillian, Josephine led a life of constant change, and at the age of 14, she saw Willie as a source of stability. He could be the family she missed so much. As the weeks slipped by, their friendship blossomed into romance.

It was during the Philadelphia engagement that an unsettling thing happened. The manager announced that the show was disbanding. Within days, each person in the cast had gone his or her separate way, and Josephine's weekly salary was a thing of the past. Marriage seemed like a safe and sensible move, and a few months later, in September 1921, Josephine married Willie Baker. All things considered, the marriage was a disappointment, but it did give Josephine one important thing: the name Baker, which she would use for the rest of her career.

After the collapse of the show in early 1921, Josephine knew she had to find work quickly. When she heard that tryouts were being held for a new, Broadway-bound musical, *Shuffle Along*, she threw on her coat and hurried to the Dunbar Theater for an audition.

Shuffle Along was a bouncy, fast-paced production, with a toe-tapping score by Noble Sissle and Eubie Blake. Containing some of the most exuberant dancing ever seen on Broadway, the show created a sensation when it opened in May 1921. *Shuffle Along*, in fact, was the first truly successful black musical, running for more than 500 performances. Like *Show Boat* (1927) and *Oklahoma!* (1943), it is considered a landmark in the history of American musical theater.

But that afternoon in Philadelphia, the future of the show was still in doubt, and Josephine stood anxiously in the wings, waiting for her chance to audition. Before she had even slipped on her tap shoes, however, she was told that she was too young to be a chorus girl. By law, she had to be 16 to appear on the New York stage. Without batting an eye, Josephine assured Noble Sissle that she was old enough, but he knew that she was lying. When she saw that it was hopeless, Josephine nodded, turned, and fighting back tears, left the theater.

Even after *Shuffle Along* had moved to Broadway and established itself as a hit, Josephine could not forget the show. Months later, when she heard that a second *Shuffle Along* company was being formed to do the road tour, she lost no time in buying a train ticket for New York, 90 miles away. Suitcase in hand, she told her husband, Willie, she would be back, though she must have hoped it would not be anytime soon.

A week later, Josephine auditioned for Al Mayer, the New York stage manager. Again, she was rejected. "Too young, too skinny," Mayer said brusquely.

This time, however, Josephine refused to take no for an answer. Again and again, she returned to the theater, never missing an audition. She was finally offered a job handling wardrobe for the *Shuffle Along* company. It was not what she wanted, but she took it anyway, because it was a step in the right direction.

A month or so later, in classic show business tradition, one of the chorus girls fell ill, and Josephine was asked to take her place. This was Josephine's big chance, and she made the most of it, stealing every scene she was in. She was quickly given a permanent spot in the show.

Josephine's appearance in the chorus of *Shuffle Along* was one of the most important events of her life. Not only was the work steady, but it gave her an opportunity to refine her comedic talents, talents that would shortly make her one of the brightest stars in vaudeville. ❧

"It's impossible to take your eyes off the little cross-eyed girl," one reviewer said of Baker's performance in The Chocolate Dandies. *"If God gave us faces, he meant us to use them,"* Josephine told her sister Margaret.

4

LA REVUE NÈGRE

TOURING WITH AN established hit such as *Shuffle Along* made life on the road a little easier for Josephine Baker. The theaters were somewhat cleaner, the orchestras were more professional, and there were even whites in the audience, who were coming to see what all the New York fuss was about. Many aspects of the tour remained the same, however: the cold hotel rooms, the loneliness, the hurried meals, the long hours spent getting from one city to another.

The racial discrimination that Baker had so vividly experienced in the South reared its ugly head again, only this time it was discrimination with a twist: It came not only from whites but from other black members of the cast. Nearly all of the chorus girls in *Shuffle Along* were light skinned, and they were proud of it. They looked down on Baker because her skin was darker than theirs. They called her "the monkey" and played cruel tricks on her, stealing her hairbrushes and gluing her shoes to the floor. It did not take long for Baker to realize that if she was ever going to get ahead, she would have to rely upon herself. No one was going to make it easy for her.

From her spot at the end of the chorus line, Baker caught the audience's attention night after night.

After October 2, 1925, when Baker made her first appearance on a Parisian stage, admirers surrounded her wherever she went. To sort out her suitors, Josephine sometimes enlisted the aid of her pet snake, Kiki. "He was adorable," she said, "just long enough to knot himself around my neck like a collar. . . . Only the bravest admirers asked me out twice, which was as good a way as any to choose among them."

37

While the rest of the girls tried their hardest to keep in step with each other, she went out of her way to look off balance, doing a crazy little dance all her own that kept the audience in stitches. She did not care if she looked clumsy or untalented. People laughed, and that was the whole point.

Baker also perfected the unusual trick of rolling each eye in a different direction at the same time. It was a strange, loony sight, and the audience burst into applause whenever she started "playin' marbles with her eyes."

In the summer of 1922, *Shuffle Along* closed on Broadway, and the New York cast itself was sent on tour. By then, Noble Sissle and Eubie Blake had heard about the "cross-eyed girl" who had become such a hit, and in August, Baker joined the main company on the road. Night after night, the houses were packed, and Baker's salary was increased to $35 a week. By now, she could dance as well as any chorus girl in the show, but she continued to stay out of step—tripping, stumbling, catching up— delighting the audience with every mistake. Her success was so singular that she toured with the main company for more than a year.

When the time came in 1924 to select the cast for Sissle and Blake's newest musical, Baker was hired immediately. The show was called *The Chocolate Dandies*, and for the first time she was given a chance to step out of the chorus and appear in several of the knockabout comedy sketches. *The Chocolate Dandies* was not a great success, but Baker received excellent reviews, and when the show closed in May 1925, she was offered a job at the Plantation Club at 50th and Broadway.

The Plantation Club was an elite night spot for New York's wealthy. Mobsters and millionaires flocked to see the club's popular revue. Baker considered it the most elegant place she had ever seen.

The waiters spoke French, the tablecloths were freshly starched, and Ethel Waters, the blues singer, was the star of the show.

Each evening, from her place in the chorus line, Baker studied Waters's mannerisms, her rich aching voice, and her dramatic choice of song material: "St. Louis Blues," "Georgia Blues," "My Man." Baker herself had a pleasing but rather thin voice; in the afternoons, while the waiters set the tables and the floor was being swept, she practiced her singing, trying to copy Waters's deep, robust sound.

The practice paid off. One evening, the star came down with a case of laryngitis, and Baker was asked to sing one of Waters's most popular songs, "Dinah." She was extremely nervous as she walked to the microphone, but the audience did not seem to notice, and at the end of the song Baker was given a tremendous round of applause. Even the chorus girls seemed genuinely excited by her success.

To no one's surprise, Ethel Waters made a speedy recovery, and the very next evening Baker found herself back in the chorus. After a short while, it became obvious that her place in the show was not ever going to get any bigger. The Plantation Club already had a star—it did not need two.

Baker had only been working at the club for a few months when her career took a surprising turn. One evening, a smartly dressed white woman came to Baker's dressing room and, extending a manicured hand, she introduced herself as Caroline Dudley. In businesslike fashion, she explained that she and a partner, André Daven, were producing a show of Negro vaudeville in Paris. She had come to America hoping to find the necessary dancers and for weeks had been visiting every nightclub and speakeasy in Harlem, the city's black district. That evening, she had caught Baker's performance and had been greatly impressed by her comic talents. Then, very casually,

Dudley asked Baker if she would like to come with her to Paris.

Needless to say, Baker was speechless. As soon as she could collect her wits, though, she realized that the offer was extremely risky. Dudley's show might fail, and Baker did not relish the idea of being stranded in a foreign country with no money and no way to get home.

There was a self-assurance about Caroline Dudley, however, that put these fears to rest. Timing, she told Baker, was everything, and in Paris the time was right for Negro vaudeville. She was certain *La Revue Nègre* would be a success.

Two factors ultimately decided Baker's future. The first, of course, was show business. Any chorus girl would have given her eyeteeth to have been in Baker's shoes. The second, and equally important, factor was discrimination. Years later, Baker captured her feelings on paper, and in doing so, she expressed the bitterness and the sadness that many black Americans were feeling at this time:

> France . . . I had dreamed of going there ever since Albert, one of the waiters at the Plantation, had shown me a photograph of the Eiffel Tower. It looked very different from the Statue of Liberty, but what did that matter? What was the good of having the statue without the liberty, the freedom to go where one chose if one was held back by one's color? No, I preferred the Eiffel Tower, which made no promises. I had sworn to myself that I would see it one day. And suddenly here was my chance.

A few weeks later, on September 15, 1925, Baker sailed for Paris aboard the SS *Berengaria*. Caroline Dudley, she learned, had chosen a total of 25 dancers and musicians for her show. As the ship pulled away from New York Harbor, Caroline chatted happily about Paris, describing in great detail the elegant theaters, the charming cafés, and the many delights of the Champs-Élysées.

To everyone's surprise, two members of the cast had been to Paris before, and Baker quickly became good friends with one of them, Sidney Bechet. A gifted clarinetist, Bechet assured her that everything was different in France, that racial discrimination was not tolerated. Baker, he said, would be treated the same as any white person. This promise of equality must have reminded her of Arthur's great dream of brotherhood.

The second night out, a gala was held for the first-class passengers. Caroline Dudley, to cut down expenses, had arranged for the troupe to perform. Unfortunately, the event proved to be Baker's first professional disaster.

Dudley suggested she dance the Charleston, but Baker refused. She wanted to be taken seriously. Remembering her success with "Dinah" at the Plantation Club, she decided to sing "Brown Eyes," a sentimental blues number. The acoustics in the large room, however, were poor, and Baker could hardly hear herself. She lost the beat a few bars into the song. Her voice cracked; she hit wrong notes. She barely managed to finish the number.

Dudley later explained to the teenager that she was too young to sing torch songs. More importantly, they were not her style. If Baker wanted to succeed in show business, Dudley told her, she would have to develop a keen sense of her strengths and weaknesses. She was a fine dancer, and she could make people laugh. Dudley encouraged her to cultivate these talents. With luck, they would make her famous.

The rest of the seven-day voyage was spent in rehearsals. Dudley worked her dancers hard, nervously watching them as they shuffled and strutted their way across the ballroom floor. *La Revue Nègre* was the first show she had ever produced, and she wondered how the Parisians would respond to the brash, enthusiastic quality of Negro vaudeville.

A founding father of jazz, clarinetist Sidney Bechet was among the troupe of black entertainers who sailed with Baker to France in 1925 to appear in La Revue Nègre. "He played so softly and sweetly," she recalled, "that tears came to my eyes."

To publicize the opening of La Revue Nègre, *Paul Colin's lively poster, which featured Baker performing the Charleston, was pasted on billboards and newsstands throughout Paris. Today, Colin's original artwork fetches high prices.*

The company arrived in Paris on the morning of September 22. It was raining lightly, and the dancers were quickly driven to the Théâtre des Champs-Élysées, a large concrete building on the avenue Montaigne. Laughing, shouting, and swinging their baggage, the troupe tap-danced across the sidewalk and into the lobby of the elegant theater.

The show, they were told, was set to open in 10 days. As the first rehearsal got under way, a young French artist named Paul Colin sat in the back row, making one quick sketch after another. It was his job to create the poster for *La Revue Nègre.* Timing was crucial: The artwork had to be at the printer the following day. Colin wanted it to be a special poster, one that would capture the knee-slapping enthusiasm of Negro dance. As he worked, his eye caught Baker as she stepped into the spotlight. Kicking out her coffee-colored legs, she began dancing a snappy Charleston. This was exactly the inspiration Colin needed. To a young Frenchman, Baker was the very essence of Harlem: exotic and colorful, and thrillingly alive.

The next day, the completed poster was rushed to the printer. It would soon appear on billboards and kiosks throughout Paris, creating tremendous controversy and excitement. The posters became so popular, in fact, that many were stolen before the show even opened.

By the end of the week, Caroline Dudley was putting the finishing touches on her colorful revue. Every afternoon, Paul Colin returned to his seat at the back of the theater to watch Baker perform her frantic Charleston. At night, he showed her the beauty of Paris by dark: the Champs-Élysées, the Arc de Triomphe, the Eiffel Tower, the intimate cafés and rollicking cabarets. In no time at all, Baker had fallen in love with the City of Light.

The thing that impressed her most about Paris was the atmosphere of total freedom. When Baker

Baker in Un Vent de Folie *in 1927. Despite her lively performance, most critics considered the show flat and predictable.*

went to a restaurant or visited the cinema, she was treated just like everyone else. She did not need to step off the sidewalk or cross the street when a white person approached, as blacks were expected to do in the United States. She could go anywhere she wanted, do anything she liked. It was a wonderful feeling; to a black American, it was almost like breathing for the first time.

Baker onstage was likened to "a dipping saxophone. Music seems to pour from her body. She grimaces, crosses her eyes, puffs her cheeks, wiggles disjointedly, does a split and finally crawls off the stage stiff-legged, her rump higher than her head, like a young giraffe."

At last, October 2 arrived—opening night. The posters had done their job: The theater was packed with excited Parisians eager to see this new form of entertainment. At 10:30 P.M., the house lights dimmed, the curtain rose, and out of the darkness, like a strange, winding serpent, came the bluesy sound of Sidney Bechet's clarinet. The melody was haunting, yet beautiful, and the Parisians were stunned. They had never heard this kind of music before—the sweet, lazy strains of Dixie—and from that moment on, *La Revue Nègre* was a total triumph.

The biggest success of the evening, however, was Baker's Charleston. Her vibrant dancing startled and amazed the French people. She was like an unleashed animal, pouncing out at the audience, catching it by surprise. As the orchestra gathered momentum, a group of bandanna-clad mammies joined Baker onstage, swiveling their hips energetically. Mesmerized, the crowd rose to its feet, and when the drummer finally smashed the cymbals, Baker somersaulted offstage to a wave of frantic applause.

Moments later, she reappeared wearing nothing but a skirt of pink feathers. In the heat of the spotlight, her beauty was breathtaking.

"Fabuleux!" people yelled. "Fabulous!"

Seized by the passion of the moment, Baker sprang into the arms of another dancer. Her entire body, she remembered, burned with feverish excitement: "Each time I leaped I seemed to touch the sky and when I regained earth it seemed to be mine alone." When the stagehands finally brought the curtain down, the response was deafening.

Clearly, Baker had taken Paris by storm. The next morning, the box office was swamped, and for the rest of the show's run, security guards were hired to control members of the audience, who sometimes rushed toward the stage as Baker was completing her dance.

One widely respected critic pronounced her "the black Venus." Another wrote that Josephine Baker had proved to the French "for the first time that black was beautiful." People began stopping her on the street, asking for her autograph. This proved to be embarrassing: Baker could hardly write her name. When flowers arrived backstage after the show, she struggled to read the simple messages inside. Still, she did her best to act like the star she now was.

With Paul Colin at her side, Baker was introduced to some of the most interesting people in the city: writers and artists, intellectuals and politicians. She visited art exhibitions, cabarets, museums, elegant parties. Little by little, she began learning her way around the vast city.

Baker's scrapbook, meanwhile, quickly filled with newspaper reviews, all of which she studied carefully. She felt her heart quicken whenever she spotted her name in the clutter of unfamiliar words. And in those late fall days of 1925, she spotted it frequently. All of Paris, it seemed, wanted to read about Josephine Baker. She was the most glorious savage the city had ever encountered. ◖◗▸

"I felt happy and free," Baker said of her early days in Paris. "Sensing that the organizers liked my work made me blossom like a flower."

5

DARK STAR

—◈—

BY THE MIDDLE of October 1925, Josephine Baker was famous, but she was also controversial. A good number of Parisians who came to see the "black Venus" stood up in the middle of her Charleston and walked out. They considered her dancing offensive and vulgar. One critic called her performance embarrassingly primitive, the jerky antics of a monkey. These barbs must have hurt the 19-year-old Baker, but as Caroline Dudley pointed out, the majority of people liked her and that was all that mattered.

As *La Revue Nègre* entered its third triumphant week, Baker began settling comfortably into her new life. With the money she was earning, she began buying beautiful clothing and expensive perfumes. Her necklace was the most unusual in Paris: a friendly snake named Kiki, who scared off more than one admirer.

Other animals quickly followed: a pig named Albert, a squawking parrot, two rabbits, a pair of goldfish. She called the pets her children and spoiled them outrageously. Her suite at the Hotel Fournet began to resemble a strange sort of zoo, a glamorous, perfume-scented barnyard. Guests had trouble finding a place to sit, but Baker refused to get rid of the animals. She was having too much fun to care what anyone thought.

Baker arrives in Vienna in 1928 to launch her first international tour. At her side is Pepito Abatino (third from left), who served as her manager for 10 years.

Every night, after performing in *La Revue Nègre*, Baker was drawn to the jazz-filled cabarets of Montmartre, a section of Paris known for its wild nightlife. One of the clubs she visited frequently was Bricktop's. A black American 12 years older than Baker, Ada "Bricktop" Smith had arrived in Paris in 1924, opening her Montmartre nightclub the same year. Jazz musician Louis Armstrong, composer Cole Porter, and writers Ernest Hemingway and John Steinbeck were among those who passed through "Brickie's" swinging doors.

As Baker's self-appointed "big sister," Bricktop introduced her to the city's tight-knit world of colored artists and musicians. There were few blacks living in Paris in the 1920s, and every now and then, they would get together for all-night jam sessions. Baker's suite at the Hotel Fournet was the scene of many wild parties, with Bricktop pouring the drinks, Baker dancing on the coffee table, and Sidney Bechet blowing the blues on a saxophone until the management came pounding on the door.

"Everything was for the moment with Josephine," Bricktop remembered. "She couldn't see past today."

After 10 weeks of sellout performances, *La Revue Nègre* went on tour to Berlin, where Baker's Charleston electrified the Germans. On opening night, the audience was so enthusiastic that Baker was lifted onto the shoulders of several men and carried offstage, applause rocking the Nelson Theatre.

During her brief stay in Berlin, Baker was introduced to Max Reinhardt, at that time the most famous director in all of Germany and Austria. Reinhardt had seen Baker in the New York cast of *Shuffle Along*, and now, watching her perform again, he asked her to become a student at his acting school. In three years' time, he said, he could turn her into a highly polished comedienne.

Baker was flattered, but she was unable to accept Reinhardt's offer. Unknown to the cast of *La Revue*

Nègre, she had already signed a contract to star at the Folies-Bergère upon her return to Paris. Though she did not know it at the time, this was a very smart career move. The Folies-Bergère was the world's most celebrated music hall, and its 1926 revue, *La Folie du Jour*, would transform Baker into something more than a star: It would turn her into a living legend.

Playing the role of Fatou, an African native, Baker slid down a painted tree and, leaping to the stage of the Folies-Bergère, she danced her way into theatrical history. Her banana-clad performance fascinated everyone, and critics exhausted their vocabulary trying to define her hypnotic appeal: She was the Black Pearl, the Creole Goddess, "the panther with the golden claws."

Fortunately for Baker, she had arrived in Paris at a time when anything associated with black culture was in vogue. Primitive art, African dance, the hot new sounds of American jazz—all were feverishly embraced by the Parisians. Though she had never been anywhere near Africa, Josephine Baker seemed to capture the violence and beauty of the jungle. Exotic and passionately alive, she was, in the words of one poet, "a mysteriously unkillable Something."

By the fall of 1926, just a few months after her scintillating opening-night performance in *La Folie du Jour*, Baker was making more money than any other entertainer in Europe. Nearly 1,000 marriage proposals arrived in the mail, and to Baker's surprise, she became one of the most photographed women in the world. Her lively Charleston was filmed and shown in theaters all over the United States. Back in St. Louis, Carrie and Arthur Martin were stunned by Tumpie's far-reaching success. In the 1920s, it was unheard of for a black woman to achieve such astonishing popularity.

Needless to say, Baker's exotic pets also received a great deal of publicity. To the annoyance of the Folies management, Baker had transformed her dress-

An energetic Baker performs her most famous dance, the Charleston.

Baker works in her office at Chez Joséphine, the cabaret she opened in December 1926. "The time was ripe," she explained. "Paris was in a giddy mood, eager for pleasure. I supplied the amusement it craved, patting my gentlemen customers' heads and pulling their beards, flattering the women and teaching them the Charleston."

ing room into something of a zoo: It was not unusual for visitors to find a boa constrictor coiled on the floor or a family of rabbits nesting in the wardrobe. The most famous of Baker's pets was a golden-eyed leopard named Chiquita. There were few sights in Paris more extraordinary than that of La Bakaire, as the French often called her, strolling down the Champs-Élysées, Chiquita on one side wearing a diamond collar, and Ethel, a chimpanzee, on the other, a choker around her neck and diamond bracelets dangling from her wrists.

On December 10, 1926, Baker opened her own nightclub on the rue Fontaine. The cabaret, Chez Joséphine, was an immediate success, attracting both Parisians and visiting Americans. Albert the pig, freshly perfumed, wandered among the tables as Baker entertained the customers with high kicks and witty jokes. Ethel the chimp wore the most stylish hats and tried to catch Baker's feathers as they flew through the air. The customers loved it, and the cabaret was packed every night.

Somehow, in the midst of all this excitement, Baker found time to write her memoirs, a surprising thing for someone who was only 20 years old. *Les Mémoires de Joséphine Baker* was published in Paris in

1927. A delightful book, it was filled with everything from reminiscences of St. Louis to soul food recipes to beauty tips. (She recommended, for instance, that women rub strawberries on their cheeks to give them better color.)

Near the end of the book, Baker pondered her future. She would continue dancing—that was certain—but she also wrote that she was tired of being a star. She wanted to get married, settle down, and have children. She sought peace, not the artificial life of the music hall.

Shortly after the book was published, however, Baker signed a contract to appear in the 1927 revue of the Folies-Bergère. *Un Vent de Folie* (A Gust of Madness) should have been a tremendous success; instead, it struck the Parisians as flat and predictable. It wasn't that Baker was different—she had as much energy as ever, and her picture was still appearing in all the newspapers. The problem was that Paris was a city constantly looking for new entertainments, and Baker's bananas were no longer new. If she was going to remain a star, she would have to pull off a difficult trick: knowing what the Parisians wanted before they knew it themselves.

That summer, Baker was asked to make her first full-length movie, *La Sirène des Tropiques* (Siren of the Tropics). It was a silly story, all about a West Indian girl falling in love with a visiting French engineer. Baker was intrigued by the project, however, and agreed to star in the silent film. Maybe this was the change she needed. . . .

It wasn't. Baker hated making the movie, finding it a boring, tiresome process. As it turned out, she was not much of an actress, and when she finally saw herself on the screen, she felt embarrassed and angry. The film, in her opinion, had been a complete waste of time.

Fortunately, her next project was much more successful: a 2-year, 25-country world tour that Baker would look back upon as a turning point in her career.

From the very start, the 1928–29 tour was filled with excitement and controversy. Baker's bananas, which had become notorious, shocked and delighted all of Europe. Her energetic dancing thrilled audiences, and in country after country, she established herself as one of the most important, most celebrated of all entertainers.

And yet Baker had failed to take one thing into consideration when setting up the tour: religion. Many of the countries included on the itinerary were predominantly Catholic, and the clergy regarded Baker as nothing short of the Devil in disguise. Her reckless life-style, banana skirt, and short hair were all regarded as sinful. As a result, Baker was frequently met at train stations by crowds of angry, sign-waving protesters.

The controversy reached its height in the Austrian city of Vienna. The idea of racial superiority, which would become a basic principle of the Nazis, who took control of Austria in 1938, was popular among the Viennese. It was easy for them to believe that Josephine Baker, a black dancer from Paris, was an inferior being, unfit to take her place in society with civilized white people.

Baker's arrival at the train station was greeted with the expected protests. As she was being driven to her hotel in a horse-drawn carriage, the entire city reverberated with the frantic pealing of bells. The churches were warning the citizens that the Devil had arrived. At St. Paul's, masses were held for the salvation of Baker's soul.

As public protest continued to swell, the city council, fearing a riot, refused to let Baker perform until it could determine what danger, if any, she presented to the people of Vienna. A month later, the Austrian parliament decided that she could

Baker with her leopard, Chiquita, the most celebrated of her pets. On one occasion, Baker took the animal to the Paris Opera, where it leaped into the orchestra pit during the performance. Reported by newspapers around the world, the incident added further sparkle to Baker's flamboyant image.

appear at the Johann Strauss Theater. The churches were packed that afternoon, as the clergy branded Baker a savage, a decadent heathen determined to corrupt their fine city. The Viennese listened, fascinated, and after the services were over, they rushed home, changed into their evening clothes, and hurried to the theater. They wanted to find out for themselves just how evil Josephine Baker really was.

They received quite a surprise. When Baker walked onstage, she was dressed not in ostrich feathers or bananas but in a beautiful cream-colored gown, buttoned at the neck. The audience gasped. Surely this could not be the Devil? Baker ignored the excited whispers and began to sing a soft lullaby, "Pretty Little Baby." Outside, she could hear the rhythmic chanting of student radicals. The drama of the moment was unforgettable.

As soon as Baker finished the song, the audience rose to its feet, cheering and shouting. Waves of applause rushed over the young star. With that one tender song, she had conquered Vienna.

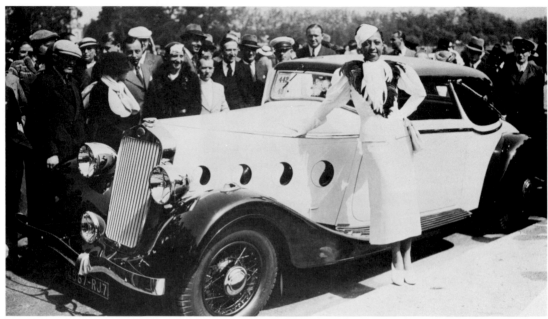

Baker shows off her fashionable new automobile—just one of the many colorful items she purchased as the highest-paid entertainer in Europe. By the time she was in her early twenties, Josephine had become, in her own words, "the toast of café society, that group of Parisians whose money flowed like champagne, whose whims made or destroyed reputations."

After three weeks of sellout performances, the tour continued on its bumpy way. In Prague, Czechoslovakia, Baker found herself caught in the middle of a riot when she arrived at the train station. This time, however, the crowd was made up not of protesters but of overexcited fans. Several train windows were shattered, and half a dozen people were injured. Seeking safety, Baker climbed onto the roof of a nearby limousine. As the car inched its way through the densely packed streets, she waved happily to the enthusiastic crowd.

Violence seemed to follow Baker wherever she went. In Budapest, the capital of Hungary, she was shocked when student protesters threw ammonia bombs onto the stage during her performance. Another evening, a young fan, hopelessly in love with Baker, shot himself after one of her concerts. In Munich, Germany, the police refused to let her perform, fearing that it would cause public disorder.

Leaving these scandals behind, Baker traveled to Spain, where she learned to dance the vigorous

zapateado and the thunderous, foot-stamping fla-
menco. In the mountain province of Huesca, she
watched in surprise as the cheering audience hurled
hundreds of shoes and hats onto the stage. She was
later told that this was their way of welcoming her to
their city.

Finally, in the summer of 1929, she sailed for
South America. Arriving in the Argentine capital of
Buenos Aires, she learned that the papers were full of
scandalous stories about her. Even President Hipólito
Irigoyen had denounced her in the press.

On opening night, hundreds of irate protesters
gathered in front of the theater. The atmosphere was
extremely tense, and the moment Baker appeared
onstage, firecrackers began exploding under the seats.
People jumped up, screaming. The musicians immediately started playing a loud tango, hoping to drown
out the noise, but they themselves were drowned out
by hysterical Argentines, who were yelling and shaking their fists in the air.

The concert was delayed for nearly half an hour
while police dragged the most violent agitators from
the hall. The smell of gunpowder was still fresh in the
air when Baker began her show. It was a nerve-
racking experience for everyone.

The rest of the South American engagements
went more smoothly. Nevertheless, Baker felt relieved when she had played the last city on the
itinerary.

All things considered, the world tour had been a
success. Yet Baker was anxious to return to Paris. She
was tired of ammonia bombs and demonstrations and
trains and ships and strange hotel rooms. She was
ready to go back to France and settle down. Her only
fear was that, after two years, the Parisians might
have forgotten her, that she would have to prove
herself all over again. The thought made her very
uneasy. ❀

6

FOLLIES

U PON RETURNING TO Paris in late 1929, Josephine Baker bought a spectacular new home. Located in the lovely suburb of Le Vésinet, 45 minutes from Paris, Le Beau-Chêne (Beautiful Oak) was a 30-room mansion with a handsome gravel driveway, a stately parade of sturdy oaks, and a magnificent garden. Baker immediately began planting rows of carrots, cabbage, and black-eyed peas. A short distance from the house, she also built a large pool surrounded by marble columns and statues of Roman goddesses. On hot days, she floated nude among the water lilies, giving press interviews and chatting casually with the neighbors.

Baker was living extravagantly; fortunately, she could afford to. At the end of 1929, when many Americans were beginning to experience the first hardships of the Great Depression, Baker's accountants informed her she was worth more than $1 million.

It was during this period that she began her long and successful collaboration with the Casino de Paris. The Casino was not as famous as the Folies-Bergère, but it was still a first-class music hall. Its seasonal productions were extremely lavish, and in no time at all, Baker reestablished herself as the leading star of the Parisian stage.

Baker at the Folies-Bergère, where several of her dance numbers were filmed in 1926 and 1927. She also starred in three feature films: La Sirène des Tropiques *(1927),* Zou-Zou *(1934), and* Princesse Tam-Tam *(1935). The last two have been successfully revived in recent years.*

Her happiest moments, though, were spent at Le Beau-Chêne. To the neighbors' surprise, Baker made a real effort to become part of the community. One by one, she got to know the local people, and whenever she heard that a family could not pay its coal bill, she quietly took care of the matter herself.

Baker also became involved in the affairs of the local orphanage. As a young woman in her twenties, she had a strong desire to become a mother, but for some reason she never bore a child. She may have been afraid that a pregnancy would change the slim, hard quality of her body. Perhaps she was unable to conceive. Whatever the reason, she now took a vital interest in the children at the nearby St. Charles Orphanage. Baker's ever-growing collection of animals delighted the youngsters, and their frequent visits to the house brought her a great deal of joy. Instead of having one or two children, she was able to open her home to dozens.

Baker would later look back on these years with great affection. At home, she was surrounded by love, and at the theater, she continued to meet the most celebrated people in Europe. The noted physicist Albert Einstein came backstage one evening and complimented Baker on her performance. The king of Siam was so excited by her dancing he offered her one of his prized elephants (one of the few animals she ever refused to accept). A particularly happy memory was the evening Noble Sissle appeared at her dressing room door. The two spent several delightful hours reminiscing about the *Shuffle Along* days.

In 1933, Baker found herself on tour once again, performing in England, Scandinavia, Belgium, Greece, Italy, and Egypt. The response was tremendous in every country. In Copenhagen, the leading newspaper called Baker "the most fantastic show lady" ever to play the Danish city, and in the opera capital of Parma, Italy, the crowd wept at her moving performance of the song "Haiti." The next morning, the enormous one-word headline said it all: DIVINA (DIVINE).

The following year, Baker surprised everyone by starring not at the Casino but in a revival of *La Créole*, a frothy operetta written by French composer Jacques Offenbach. At first, Baker was afraid she would be unable to sing the demanding role of the West Indian girl. Classical music, after all, was hardly her area of expertise. The challenge proved irresistible, however, and Baker managed to turn in a delightful performance. *La Créole* became so popular, in fact, that on one occasion it was transmitted by radio to England. "How incredible to think that my voice had crossed the Channel!" Baker later wrote.

Her voice would soon be crossing the Atlantic. Much to her surprise, Baker was invited to appear in the 1936 version of the *Ziegfeld Follies*. Florenz Ziegfeld, the legendary theatrical producer, had died in 1932, and the New York show was now being produced by Jake and Lee Shubert. Like all the *Ziegfeld Follies*, the 1936 production promised to be spectacular: Vincente Minnelli was designing the sets and costumes, Ira Gershwin was penning the lyrics, Vernon Duke was writing the score, and the popular comedienne Fanny Brice would be the headliner of the show. Two other cast members, Bob Hope and Eve Arden, would go on to become major stars. Clearly, Baker was in good company.

The thought of returning to America after 10 years was intimidating, but Baker realized it was an important career move. Additionally, she saw the *Follies* as an opportunity to further the black cause. By appearing onstage with Fanny Brice, she hoped to prove to American audiences that it did not matter if a person was black or white—what mattered was the talent, not the color.

Baker was setting herself up for a bitter disappointment. Ten years and several thousand miles separated the 29-year-old entertainer from her native

Baker receives top billing in an advertisement for the Folies-Bergère. "I was drawn, painted, sketched, caricatured, photographed, filmed," she recalled. During this period, she also cut dozens of popular records.

Baker onstage in the 1936 Broadway production of the Ziegfeld Follies. The New York critics were not impressed. "Miss Baker has refined her art until there is nothing left in it," complained one reviewer.

country; apparently, she had forgotten how deeply the roots of discrimination were embedded in American society.

Baker sailed aboard the French liner *Normandie* in September 1935. Later, she would claim that Ziegfeld's widow, film star Billie Burke, happened to be on the same voyage. According to Baker, she sent Burke an invitation suggesting they have dinner together. When Burke made her appearance in the large dining room, however, she stared at Baker coldly, turned on her heel, and left without a word. One can only assume the snub was racially motivated. In any event, it was the first in a series of cruel moments that poisoned Baker's return to America.

Upon arriving in New York City, she checked into the Hotel St. Moritz, where the manager informed Baker that because she was black, she would have to use the servants' entrance. The fact that Baker was a *Follies* star made no difference. Many of the guests were from the South, the manager explained, and the sight of a black woman in the lobby might offend them. It was an embarrassing situation, but Baker decided not to make a fuss. She knew it would be bad publicity for the show.

Before her rehearsals began, Baker was able to spend five days visiting her family in St. Louis. Since her departure in 1925, Grandma McDonald and Arthur Martin had both died. Arthur's last few years had been tragic. His fierce temper and frequent bouts of depression finally resulted in mental illness. Carrie had him committed to the city asylum, where he died in 1934.

Upon leaving St. Louis, Baker made a quick visit to Chicago, where she informed her husband, Willie Baker, that she wanted a divorce. Josephine and Willie were strangers by now; they had not seen each other in 10 years, and both agreed that it was foolish to continue the marriage. After signing the necessary papers, Josephine hurried back to New York, where the *Follies* rehearsals were already under way.

Sadly, the next few weeks were the most discouraging of Baker's professional career. Not only did the stars ignore her, but the *Follies* management treated her like a child, insisting they knew what was best for her. Baker tried to stay agreeable, but her mood turned sour when she realized she had only a small role in the show. Fanny Brice was given all the best scenes, and Bob Hope, a former boxer, was allowed to introduce the show's most memorable song, "I Can't Get Started with You." Baker, on the other hand, appeared onstage only four times.

What angered her most, though, was that she was not allowed to wear the outfits she had brought with her from Paris. Vincente Minnelli's costumes were undeniably beautiful, but they were not the costumes Baker wanted to wear. One creation, a gold mesh evening gown, weighed nearly 100 pounds. It was stunning to look at, but impossible to perform in.

"I could tell from the start that I'd never make it," Baker wrote. "I had been overglamorized, hopelessly type-cast."

She was not surprised, therefore, when the critics panned her opening-night performance. Her voice, they said, was too thin and "dwarf-like" to fill the spacious Winter Garden Theater. It confused and annoyed New Yorkers to hear a black woman speak with a French accent, and Baker was immediately labeled a "foreigner." Even her celebrated banana dance fell flat. *Time* magazine was unusually harsh, dismissing the "Negro wench . . . whose dancing and singing might be topped practically anywhere outside of Paris."

Praise was lavished, however, on Fanny Brice, Bob Hope, Eve Arden, and especially Vincente Minnelli. It disappointed and angered Baker that she could not share in their success. She eventually told

Back in Paris after her discouraging appearance in the Ziegfeld Follies, Baker gives a free concert on the city streets. "I could tell from the start that I'd never make it," she said of the Follies. "There was no room to be myself; I had been overglamorized, hopelessly type-cast."

Jake and Lee Shubert that she wanted to leave the *Follies*; and being smart businessmen, they quickly released her from her contract. She was replaced by burlesque star Gypsy Rose Lee.

Sadder but wiser, Baker returned to France, where she headlined the 1937 revue of the Folies-Bergère, *En Super Folies*. She also reopened her cabaret, Chez Joséphine, spending her midnights singing and dancing for the crowds of tourists attending the 1937 Colonial Exposition. The situation was ironic: The Americans who had disliked her at home could not seem to get enough of her in Paris. Increasingly, Baker felt that she and America were simply not compatible, and not long after her return to Paris, she legally became a French citizen. Now, she felt, she truly belonged.

It was also in early 1937 that Baker fell in love. The man in question was a handsome Jewish millionaire named Jean Lion. Ambitious and clever, Lion had made his fortune in the sugar market, and Baker was dazzled by his good looks and sophisticated charm. He, in turn, was impressed by her energy and exuberant personality. He was even more impressed by Baker's popularity with the French people. At the age of 27, Lion was considering a career in politics, and he sensed immediately that a woman like Baker could open many doors for him.

Both shared a passion for outdoor sports, and in the spring of 1937, they filled their days with horseback riding, fox hunting, sight-seeing, and racing through the French countryside in expensive automobiles. They even flew airplanes together, a sport that obsessed Baker. Whenever she had an hour to spare, she rushed to the airport, and in no time at all was doing loop-the-loops over the Versailles Palace.

It was during one such plane ride, in fact, that Jean Lion proposed to Baker. She accepted immediately. At the age of 31, she feared her youth was passing, and with it her chances of raising a family. A new career as Madame Lion would not only be secure but wonderfully romantic—or so Baker believed. Like many stars, she had convinced herself that what she really wanted was a quiet life out of the spotlight. She did not realize how important fame had become to her.

The wedding was held that fall in Lion's hometown of Crèvecoeur-le-Grand, a hamlet northwest of Paris. On the day of the ceremony, hundreds of people filled the town square. After Baker and Lion exchanged their vows, cheers went up, trumpets were blown, and shotguns were fired ceremoniously into the air. Baker was thrilled.

"I want to be a housewife and have at least six children," she told the press, a plan which her husband supported wholeheartedly.

Baker was undoubtedly speaking from the heart, and if she had been willing to sacrifice her career, her third marriage might have lasted. Instead, it was doomed from the start. In his own way, Jean was a celebrity in Parisian society, a handsome playboy who was not used to sharing the spotlight with anyone. Now that he and Baker were married, he expected her to become a traditional wife. As an aristocrat, he relied upon her to plan dinner parties, write tasteful thank-you notes, and arrange charity teas. In public, Baker was expected to be well dressed, well read, and well spoken. In short, her job was to make her husband look powerful and successful.

It was a role Baker was not used to playing. She tried her best to become a society hostess, but she never felt comfortable. She was used to having people surround *her*, and the idea of existing for someone else was not entirely pleasant. Baker respected and loved Lion, but she was not willing to become his shadow. Naturally, this created tension between them. Also, with Baker's hectic schedule, she and Jean were not able to spend as much time together as they would have liked. He worked during the day, she worked at night. It was a lonely combination for newlyweds.

Finally, Lion asked her to quit show business. Baker knew it was the only way she could save her marriage, and hoping to begin a family, she agreed to retire. First, however, she insisted on a farewell tour. Jean grudgingly gave his approval.

The tour was difficult in more ways than one. The atmosphere in Europe in the late 1930s was becoming increasingly tense. Adolf Hitler had seized power in Germany in 1933, and by 1935 his plans to establish the German people as the "master race" were beginning to take shape. Claiming to be a man of peace, Hitler was in reality a ruthless dictator determined to create a new world order. He despised the Soviet system of bolshevism, considered France a

dire enemy, and regarded all Jewish people as evil. His book *Mein Kampf* (My Struggle) was the bible of the growing Nazi party.

As the rest of Europe watched apprehensively, Germany allied itself with Italy in 1936. Soon after, it did the same with Japan. The real aggression began in 1938, when Hitler's troops occupied Austria. Baker at that time was just beginning her farewell tour, and the increasing rumors of war deeply worried her. What if the Nazis invaded France? As a black French citizen and the wife of a Jew, she knew she would be shown no mercy by Adolf Hitler's "master race."

Lion accompanied her on the early part of the tour, but business concerns eventually took him back to France, where the government situation was very shaky. Baker continued the tour alone, and with

"I teel you how I fly zee plane, how I have learn zee loop-zee-loop. I love eet! I thrill eet!" Baker told writer Langston Hughes during an interview in 1937. She was one of the first celebrities to travel by private plane, but unlike other stars, she did most of the piloting herself.

Baker finishes first in a horse race outside Paris. "The most sensational woman anybody ever saw," author Ernest Hemingway said of her. "Or ever will."

every passing week, she realized how much she truly loved performing. She felt most alive when she was onstage, basking in the admiration of excited crowds. Berlin, Warsaw, Nice, Zurich, London . . . the longer the tour lasted, the more reluctant she was to go home.

Finally, Lion lost his temper. He demanded that Baker abandon her career and return to Paris. Not surprisingly, she refused. Baker now had to make an extremely difficult decision. She still loved Jean, but after a great deal of soul-searching, she had to admit that she loved her career more. Ironically, it was at this time that she discovered she was pregnant. She continued the tour, however, and was beginning to knit a colorful collection of baby clothes when she suffered a sudden miscarriage.

"I lost the only thing that could have bound Jean and me together," Baker wrote. After less than a year of marriage, the Lions decided to separate.

Meanwhile, the wheels of war were beginning to turn faster. One of Hitler's basic beliefs was that the Jews were an impure people who were poisoning the Aryan race. He felt they must be dealt with sharply, and on November 9, 1938, the shops and homes of Jewish families throughout Germany were stoned and burned to the ground. Thousands of windows were shattered as chanting Nazi youths ran through the streets. The Night of Broken Glass, as it came to be called, shocked all of Europe. When Baker heard of the persecution and the rioting, she quickly joined the International League Against Racism and Anti-Semitism. She was not sure how she could help, but joining the League gave her a sense of confidence that, in time, would prove invaluable.

Less than 10 months later, on September 1, 1939, Hitler's troops invaded Poland. Britain and France immediately issued declarations of war. The United States tried to stay neutral, but the truth could no longer be avoided: World War II had begun. ❧

7

THE RESISTANCE

FEELING THE NEED to help the war effort in some way, Josephine Baker joined the Red Cross. The need for volunteers was great, and she spent several hours every day at the busy center, putting together boxes of food, finding housing for homeless families, and ladling out soup for the lines of hungry people. In the evenings, when she was not performing with noted entertainer Maurice Chevalier at the Casino de Paris, she appeared at charity functions, always ready to sing and dance to raise money for the Allied cause.

In the spring of 1940, the war began to escalate. On April 9, Hitler's troops occupied the neutral territories of Norway and Denmark, and there was widespread fear that France might be invaded next. "It became the custom to bolt the shutters and to black out the lights and everyone got used to waiting," Chevalier wrote.

The Casino de Paris closed its doors at the end of May. Now, Baker pushed herself harder than ever, spending six days a week at the Red Cross center. On the seventh, she flew much-needed supplies across the border to Belgium. It did not take long for her patriotism to attract the notice of the French military

Sublieutenant Baker in the uniform of the Women's Auxiliary of the Free French Air Force. The French government awarded her the high rank in appreciation of her secret intelligence work and propaganda efforts during World War II.

police. One of its top officers, Jacques Abtey, quietly visited Baker at Le Beau-Chêne; he wanted to know if she would be willing to become an undercover agent for the Allied forces. Baker was surprised, and deeply honored, to receive such an invitation.

Abtey's reason for approaching Baker was simple. As a well-known entertainer, she had access to important people and could come and go as she pleased. As long as she was discreet, she would not be suspected. Baker knew that the job could be dangerous, even fatal, but she assured Abtey that she was prepared to give her life for her adopted country. In France, she explained, she had discovered the meaning of true freedom, and she would now do anything to protect it.

That afternoon, Abtey reported the good news to his commanding officer: Josephine Baker was officially a member of the French Resistance.

Less is known about Baker's wartime activities than about any other part of her life. She herself was always reluctant to discuss this period; even 30 years after the war had ended, she still felt the need to be discreet. The French Resistance had undoubtedly sworn her to secrecy during those gloomy spring days of 1940.

Once recruited into the underground movement, Baker was put through a series of rigid tests. She learned how to handle a pistol and within weeks was able to shoot the flame off a candle at 20 yards. She also learned karate, a Japanese form of self-defense. She was drilled in German and Italian until she could speak and read both languages comfortably. She was also put through a series of challenging memory tests. As Abtey explained, there would be instances when she would have to remember information for weeks, even months, at a time.

Finally, at the end of her training, Baker was given a handful of cyanide pills. Abtey told her that if she ever found herself in a situation she could not

handle, the capsules killed instantly. Suicide, the Resistance believed, was a noble alternative to enemy capture.

Baker's first assignment was accomplished with surprising ease. As a popular entertainer, she was on friendly terms with several high-ranking officials of the Italian government, including Benito Mussolini, the ruler of Italy. Within a matter of days, she successfully obtained some valuable information—possibly a codebook—that she passed on to Abtey.

Baker's career as an undercover agent had just begun when the Germans occupied Paris on June 13. Along with thousands of other terrified citizens, Baker fled the city, which fell to the enemy without a single shot being fired. Nazi flags unfurled triumphantly from the windows as German troops marched in front of the Eiffel Tower.

"Those who stayed in the city lived in a kind of nightmare," Maurice Chevalier remembered. "We just tried to hang on and do our job the best we could."

Baker, meanwhile, was driving south as quickly as she could. Her destination was not Le Beau-Chêne, which was too close for comfort, but Les

Early in World War II, Baker and entertainer Maurice Chevalier took their Casino de Paris revue on the road and staged shows to boost the morale of French troops on the front lines. Baker also held benefit performances to aid war victims.

Milandes, a spacious, 50-room château she had rented in 1938. Baker had fallen in love with the house the moment she saw it, but she had never been able to spend more than a few days there. Much later, Les Milandes would play a significant role in her life. In the summer of 1940, however, she saw it as little more than a safe refuge from the Nazis.

In July, Abtey joined Baker at the château, and together they spent the next few months hiding nervous refugees and listening to uncertain reports over the radio. In this way, they learned that the Germans had occupied only part of France. There were now two zones, northern and southern, the second of which was still held by the French. How long this division would last no one could say.

As fall approached, Baker continued to shelter as many people as she could, but it was a risky situation. Anyone sympathetic to the Nazis could turn her in for a hefty reward. She was relieved, therefore, when she and Abtey received orders from Resistance head-quarters instructing them to travel to the neutral territory of Lisbon, Portugal. There, Abtey would make contact with members of the British intelli-gence.

For the next eight months, Baker and Abtey worked tirelessly for the French Resistance. Their assignments were difficult, and often dangerous, but they were very successful at what they did.

As Abtey had hoped, Baker was able to travel across borders easily—something he would have had trouble doing on his own. Whenever anyone asked why she was traveling so much, Baker gave the simple excuse that she was on tour. To make every-thing look legitimate, she brought along many pieces of luggage and a colorful assortment of pets, including two monkeys and a Great Dane. Abtey, carefully disguised, was usually introduced as her secretary.

Baker's "tour" was exciting, exotic, and exhaust-ing. Even after coming down with pneumonia, she refused to let herself rest. Lisbon, Marseilles, London, Algiers, Barcelona, Madrid . . . in every city, Baker was invited to embassy functions and high society parties. Because these events were usually filled with government officials, she attended them all, eavesdropping on the conversations around her. Later, locked in her hotel room, she carefully wrote down everything she had heard, her invisible-ink pen racing across her sheet music.

As a celebrity, Baker was rarely subjected to border searches—more often than not, she and Abtey were simply waved through customs. In many ways, they were a perfect team, and the information they collected was very valuable to the French Resistance.

In June 1941, however, Baker's luck ran out. She developed an infection, and, because she was still recovering from pneumonia, her condition swiftly turned critical. Years later, she would claim that the Nazis had poisoned her with cyanide. In any event, her illness was so serious that she had to spend the next 19 months slowly recovering in Casablanca, a port city in Morocco.

At first, when Baker appeared to be making little, if any, progress, Abtey stayed by her side constantly. Concerned friends and well-wishers visited her daily at the Mers Sultan clinic. Many of these visitors were Resistance members, and secret meetings were frequently held at her bedside. Usually, Baker was too weak to follow the hushed conversations.

As time went on, a painful case of peritonitis set in. Blood poisoning followed, and no less than three operations were performed in an effort to save Baker's life. For months, she remained delirious, her body shaking with fever. The rumor soon spread that she had died, and her obituary promptly appeared in newspapers throughout the world.

It was not until March 1943 that Baker felt strong enough to leave the hospital. The war was still going

Baker in the uniform of a U.S. Air Force lieutenant. Even though most American troops were racially segregated during World War II, she insisted that black soldiers be allowed to sit with whites whenever she performed. "In order to present a united front to the enemy," she said, "we would have to be true allies, oblivious of color and origins."

on, and to her dismay, all of France was now occupied by the Germans. It did not appear that the fighting would end anytime soon.

Before leaving Casablanca, Baker was invited to perform at the Liberty Club, a canteen where black and white soldiers could mingle socially. It had been two years since Baker had appeared onstage, but knowing how much the concert would mean to the men, she accepted the invitation. Hundreds of American soldiers turned out for the event; many could not fit inside the canteen and scrambled onto the roof to hear the music through the air vents.

The Liberty Club concert was a turning point in Baker's career. She looked extremely thin and her stomach was still swathed in bandages, but clearly, she had lost none of her old enthusiasm. As she entertained the men with a Gershwin tune, she felt a wonderful energy filling her body. The 20 minutes Baker spent onstage were more beneficial to her recovery than the interminable months she had spent in the hospital. When the concert ended, the soldiers jumped to their feet, cheering and applauding loudly. It was one of the warmest, most exciting ovations Baker had ever received, and it helped determine her future participation in the war.

Baker now informed Jacques Abtey she wanted to go on tour again—a *real* tour, this time. Her performance at the canteen had convinced her that the Allied soldiers desperately needed entertainment. Naturally, her doctors discouraged the idea, but Baker's mind was made up. She would do everything she could to help the Allied forces. Anything less, she felt, would be unpatriotic.

Abtey agreed to accompany her, and within weeks the details had been arranged. Baker was on the road again, only this time there was one stipulation: Wherever she performed, she insisted that the black soldiers be allowed to sit with the whites.

Usually, blacks were forced to stand in the back, a custom Baker tried to abolish.

In 1943, this simple request was considered controversial. The American army, which was segregated according to race, bristled at the idea that a black Frenchwoman was attempting to change its long-standing policy. Nevertheless, Baker believed it was absolutely necessary that blacks and whites be treated equally in the army. She saw no point in waging war on Hitler if discrimination was allowed to exist on the battlefield.

Not every U.S. Army official agreed with Baker, but she was usually given her way. It was a small, but significant, step forward in the fight against racism.

For the next year and a half, Baker entertained American, British, and French forces throughout North Africa and the Middle East. As usual, she drove herself to the point of exhaustion, never complaining and never accepting any pay for her work. She saw herself as simply another soldier doing her duty for her country.

The conditions under which Baker performed were frequently dangerous and never luxurious. Material for clothing, for instance, was hard to come by during the war, and many of Baker's costumes were hastily assembled from pieces of spare cloth. She rarely performed in theaters, usually singing and dancing on a few boards stretched across empty oil drums. Evening performances were lit by military searchlights. More than once, Baker had to drop to the stage in the middle of a song as German aircraft appeared overhead, spraying bullets into the crowd.

Traveling from one military camp to another presented its own difficulties. Maps were unreliable, the heat could be excruciating, violent sandstorms made progress slow, and fresh water was scarce. Sleeping was often impossible: The night air was extremely cold, and sand fleas infested the bedrolls.

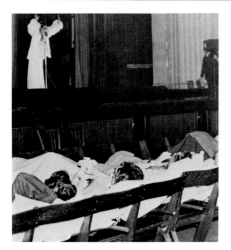

Baker entertains wounded former prisoners of war at a London hospital in 1945. By this time, her own health was far from perfect: Struck gravely ill in mid-1941, she had taken 19 months to recover.

Starving jackals and coyotes were a constant menace.

Baker never lost her courage, however, keeping up her spirits wherever she went. To the French soldiers stationed in the searing Libyan desert, she was like an uncorked bottle of champagne, bubbling and exotic. When she danced the Charleston, it was a delightful reminder of prewar Paris. When she sang the "Marseillaise," the French national anthem, it was a sobering reminder of the ongoing struggle for liberty. The men, most of whom had never heard of Josephine Baker before, cheered themselves hoarse at every performance.

By mid-1944, the Allies appeared to be winning the war. A disgraced Mussolini had resigned as the leader of Italy; Allied bombs were raining upon Germany; and Hitler's efforts to occupy Russia had completely failed. On June 6, the Americans and the British invaded France, and by August, Paris had been liberated. People wept joyfully as the Allied soldiers rode through the crowded streets.

Baker returned home, but stayed only long enough to reorganize the tour, which would now focus on countries that had already been liberated. Leaving Paris, she took with her a French bandleader she had met in the early 1930s, Jo Bouillon, and together they performed at numerous benefits, raising more than a million francs for war victims. Bouillon's admiration for Baker grew steadily as he watched her tour the army camps and visit the hospitals, comforting the wounded. He was especially moved when she distributed Christmas presents to the poor—gifts she had purchased by pawning her jewelry.

By April 1945, Germany was on the brink of collapse. Italy had long since surrendered to the Allies; the British were sweeping across northern Germany; and the Russians had surrounded the capital city of Berlin. Hitler, in his desperation, realized that he had been defeated, and on April 30 he committed suicide in his Berlin bunker. After nearly six long years, the European war was over.

Baker and Jo Bouillon were touring when the good news was announced, and they made arrangements to return to Paris as quickly as possible. As their ship made its way toward France, Baker began to think about her future. Now that the war was over, there was no longer any need to entertain the troops. Her career as a Resistance agent was also finished.

Bouillon suggested that Baker go on tour again. It was an idea for which the 38-year-old entertainer felt little enthusiasm. Somehow, she felt she should do something more significant, more valuable than simply accept another round of concert engagements. During the war, Baker had discovered a deep need within herself to help other people. She did not see how she could satisfy this need by dancing in bananas again.

The tour was arranged, however, and Baker spent the early months of 1946 appearing in major cities throughout Europe and North Africa. In every country, she was as popular as ever. Yet she still felt the need to do something more important, more lasting. Baker's heart was restless.

That summer, while performing in Casablanca, a sharp pain seized her stomach. Within hours, Baker was seriously ill. Two emergency operations were performed, and to her deep disappointment she once again found herself confined to the hospital.

Baker was still in her sickbed, in fact, when she received from the French government the distinguished Medal of the Resistance with Rosette for her patriotism during the war. As the medal was pinned to her hospital gown that October afternoon, she felt extremely proud and, at the same time, a little wistful. She wondered if she would ever again find another cause that would give her the satisfaction and pride she had known during the war. ❦

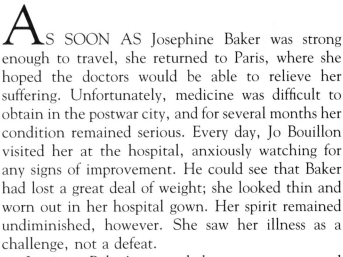

8

SIMPLE TRUTHS

A S SOON AS Josephine Baker was strong
enough to travel, she returned to Paris, where she
hoped the doctors would be able to relieve her
suffering. Unfortunately, medicine was difficult to
obtain in the postwar city, and for several months her
condition remained serious. Every day, Jo Bouillon
visited her at the hospital, anxiously watching for
any signs of improvement. He could see that Baker
had lost a great deal of weight; she looked thin and
worn out in her hospital gown. Her spirit remained
undiminished, however. She saw her illness as a
challenge, not a defeat.

In time, Baker's strength began to return, and
with it, her appetite. Gradually, color was restored to
her pale cheeks. Nevertheless, recovery was a slow
and tedious process. To pass the time, Baker began
thinking once again about her future. Bouillon sat by
her bedside, listening for hours to her plans. Her first
and most important goal was to raise a family. At the
age of 40, Baker knew her childbearing years were
coming to an end. Adoption, therefore, was the
logical solution. As soon as she was well, she hoped
to begin visiting the local orphanages.

*Baker back onstage at the Folies-Bergère in February 1949. She
left the show seven months later to open Les Milandes, her
country home in southern France, as a tourist resort and
educational center.*

Jo Bouillon also had dreams. A talented band-leader, he had just been appointed director of a popular cabaret in Paris. Thanks to his radio program, his name was becoming well known in the city's music circles. It was obvious Jo Bouillon was going places.

By the spring of 1947, he and Baker had fallen in love. When Bouillon asked for her hand in marriage, Baker happily agreed. After the confusion of the war, she was eager to settle down and begin raising a family.

One sunny afternoon, Baker and Bouillon drove to Les Milandes, the 15th-century château where she and Jacques Abtey had spent the early months of 1940 hiding refugees. The castlelike home was located in the Dordogne Valley, a beautiful rocky region in the southern part of France.

For hours, Baker poked through the drafty rooms and wandered through the overgrown garden. Nearby, the Dordogne River wound its lazy way northward. There was a quiet, unhurried feeling to the estate, and by the end of the afternoon, Baker had decided that it would be at Les Milandes that she and Jo would raise their adopted children.

To her delight, the owners were willing to sell the secluded property. In order to raise the necessary money, Baker sold her five-story townhouse in Paris where she had lived with Jean Lion. She also made arrangements to sell Le Beau-Chêne, her château in Le Vésinet.

As time passed, Baker's plans for the estate began to broaden. She wanted not only to make Les Milandes her home—she hoped to turn it into a tourist resort, a vacation getaway for city dwellers. The setting was rugged and beautiful; to make it even more attractive, she decided to build a swimming pool, a restaurant, and a small zoo.

Baker's plan was charming, but it would take a great deal of money to turn the unheated, crumbling château into a popular attraction. That meant only one thing: She would have to go on tour again.

Baker and Bouillon were married in the stone chapel at Les Milandes on June 3, 1947. Following the simple ceremony, there was singing and dancing and the cutting of a spectacular five-foot wedding cake. Baker was in wonderful spirits that day. It happened to be her 41st birthday, and she felt tremendously optimistic about the future. If all went well, the profits from her upcoming tour would allow construction to begin at Les Milandes before the end of the year.

Unfortunately, the 1947–48 world tour was extremely rocky. Baker's concerts in Europe and South America were highly successful, but in Havana, Cuba, she encountered a problem. Arriving at the hotel where Jo had made their reservations, the couple were informed that there were no rooms available. Baker immediately suspected she was being turned away because she was black.

Eleven years earlier, when she had been forced to use the servants' entrance at a New York hotel, Baker had accepted the situation. Blacks and whites simply did not mix in prewar society. Now, feeling an angry pride rise within her, she decided to fight back. Upon leaving the hotel in Havana, she contacted a lawyer and filed a formal complaint. The local papers, sniffing out the story, requested interviews, which Baker granted. Answering the reporters' questions helped her solidify her ideas about racism.

Baker stayed in Havana for a total of three months, speaking out against discrimination wherever she went. As a well-known entertainer, she had one distinct advantage: Her name could draw a crowd. She used this advantage time and again to further her controversial cause.

Baker's ideas were simple yet effective. She believed that all people were created equal, and that blacks and whites could live together peacefully. At

Baker with her fourth husband, orchestra leader Jo Bouillon, who claimed that "Josephine had swept into my life like a whirlwind." They were married in 1947.

*Baker welcomes her mother,
Carrie, to France in 1948.
"Mama was the only person my
sister heeded," noted Josephine's
sister Margaret, who had arrived
with Carrie to live at Les
Milandes.*

public gatherings, she vividly described episodes from her own life: the night of terror when Boxcar Town burned; the *Shuffle Along* cast making fun of her because of her dark skin; her arrival in Vienna, the church bells warning the citizens that the Devil had arrived. These memories, and others, gave Baker's speeches a painful urgency that was difficult to ignore. The people of Havana were deeply moved and quickly formed the Association of Friends of Josefina. Its symbol, appropriately, was two hearts intertwined.

By the time Baker left for North America, her Cuban activities had been well publicized in the United States. One by one, theater owners began canceling her engagements—she was too political for their tastes. Baker refused to yield to the financial pressure, however. She believed the fight for justice was more important than money. Gradually, she began to see herself as a spokesperson for all oppressed minorities.

At Fisk University, a black college in Nashville, Tennessee, Baker lectured on the subject of "Racial Equality in France." The students seemed eager to listen, but at the same time they were wary of anyone who tried to change the system, fearful that things might only get worse. This fear, which led to the acceptance of injustice, saddened Baker. Social change, she learned, was a slow and painful process.

In New York City, it was nearly impossible to find a hotel that would allow Baker to stay under its roof for more than one night. Again and again, she and Jo were told to pack their bags and leave.

In effect, Baker was being forced out of the country. Yet there was little she could do to change the situation. This kind of treatment was the bitter price she had to pay for her controversial beliefs.

Deeply discouraged, Baker returned to France in February 1948. There, she began the enormous task of turning Les Milandes into a tourist center. Hardly taking time to unpack, she began contacting architects, gardeners, electricians, plumbers, and carpenters. Soon, the sleepy château was buzzing with activity. Fences were thrown up, cement was poured, geraniums were planted, and one by one, Baker's animals began to arrive. Monkeys, parrots, dogs, cats, mice, peacocks—all found their way to the old château in the Dordogne Valley.

Because the world tour had not raised the money Baker had expected, it was necessary for her to continue making personal appearances. These concert engagements frequently took her out of France, but she did not lose heart. Every appearance, she knew, would bring Les Milandes one step closer to completion.

After 19 months of continuous work, the château was ready for its grand opening on September 4, 1949. The event had been well publicized, and Baker was hoping that at least 1,500 people would attend. She was delighted, and a little stunned, when 10,000 showed up, eager to take part in the celebration. All afternoon, families bowled on the lawn, ran footraces, visited the animals, relaxed under the trees, rode bicycles, and listened to Baker sing on the little stage erected in the pleasure garden. As the sun slipped over the horizon and darkness fell, fireworks lit up the sky.

Later, when everyone had gone home and Jo had totaled up the receipts, Baker was delighted to see that they had raised more than a quarter of a million francs. Now, they could afford to put in a soccer field and start digging the swimming pool. . . .

No matter how much money they made, however, it never seemed to be enough. Baker's plans for improving the château were so costly that touring became a way of life for her. Switzerland, Spain, Holland, Germany, North Africa . . . there must have been moments when Baker felt she was trapped in a vicious circle. To support Les Milandes, she had to stay on tour, and by doing so, she was rarely able to enjoy what she worked so hard to create.

By 1951, Baker was performing in the United States again, where she dazzled everyone with her dramatic singing, sensational dancing, and—last but not least—her $150,000 wardrobe. In San Francisco, the critics made no attempt to restrain their enthusiasm; she was, in their opinion, "the most exciting thing to hit [the city] since the Golden Gate Bridge."

There was, simultaneously, an aura of controversy surrounding Baker's tour. People were discovering that La Bakaire was a bold woman, unafraid to speak her mind on the sensitive issue of discrimination. Naturally, this worried many theater managers, who preferred to cancel her engagements rather than deal with outraged white customers. White supremacist groups such as the Ku Klux Klan threatened her on numerous occasions, but Baker refused to back down. As she explained to the press, she was demanding nothing more than the basic rights "granted to any other citizen of this country."

In Miami, Florida, where discrimination was quietly enforced, Baker was informed that blacks were too afraid to come to the all-white Copa City, where she was scheduled to perform. Faced with this challenge, she spent the next two days driving through the black neighborhoods, assuring the people that they had every civil right to attend her show.

On opening night, the black community turned out in droves. Seeing so many of them sitting in the audience, Baker's eyes grew teary. "I can't express my joy," she told the crowd. "This is a very significant occasion for us, and by 'us' I mean the *entire human race*."

In city after city, Baker made a point of visiting retail stores, chambers of commerce, and local industries. At each stop, she encouraged employers to hire

A high point of Baker's dazzling nightclub act in 1951 was her fashionable wardrobe, which included 13 outfits by the world's top designers. She also captivated the audience with her ability to sing in English, French, German, Italian, Portuguese, and Yiddish.

more blacks. In San Francisco, she made an appointment to see Frank Teasdale, the president of Oakland's Key System Transit Company. Their meeting was tense.

"You mean to tell me that Negroes who managed to drive army trucks during the war aren't qualified to drive your city buses?" she asked.

Teasdale tried to tell her that the policy was not his to change, but Baker could see she was wasting her time and walked out of the office.

In every theater and nightclub where she performed, Baker made sure that black stagehands and musicians were hired. She also refused to accept engagements in any city where blacks could not stay in the first-class hotels. Atlanta, therefore, was dropped from the itinerary.

In Los Angeles, Baker went so far as to have a Texan arrested for calling her a "nigger" in a restaurant. In court, she insisted her civil rights had been violated. The judge agreed, and the man was fined $100.

The highlight of Baker's tour occurred in New York City on May 20, 1951. On that day, the National Association for the Advancement of Colored People (NAACP) named her the Most Outstanding Woman of the Year and sponsored Josephine Baker Day in Harlem. Despite the wet weather, 100,000 people turned out for the gala event. As the 27-car parade snaked its way down Seventh Avenue, thousands of blacks leaned out their windows and hung from fire escapes to see for themselves the courageous Frenchwoman who was fighting so hard to end discrimination.

In retrospect, Baker's tour of the United States was a remarkable example of how one person could change the thinking of many in a practical, nonviolent way. Her direct manner of speaking impressed people, and by late 1951, she was seen as something of a heroine, a woman who spoke simple truths from the heart.

Then, in one disastrous evening, it all came apart.

On the night of October 16, Baker performed at the Roxy Theater in New York City. After finishing her show, she and a few friends decided to have dinner at the popular Stork Club on East 53rd Street. Though it was understood that the exclusive club was for whites only, Baker was admitted without comment. She took her seat at one of the tables and ordered a light dinner.

Forty-five minutes later, Baker was still waiting for her meal. Though service at the Stork Club was often slow, Baker suspected she was being discriminated against. Finally, she collared a waiter and

Treated like a chief of state, Baker (wearing a custom-made white Christian Dior dress) rides in a 27-car parade as part of the Josephine Baker Day celebration in Harlem. The festivities, which took place on May 20, 1951, also included, according to Jo Bouillon, "a huge luncheon, an even bigger cocktail party, a ball. . . . Josephine sailed through it all, stopping only to change clothes."

asked him where her steak was. A bit flustered, he told her the restaurant was out of steak. Baker was convinced the man was lying.

Determined to beat the restaurant at its own game, Baker inquired in a steady voice about the crabmeat cocktail she had also ordered. Conversations had hushed, meanwhile, and people were beginning to turn in her direction.

The waiter seemed anxious to leave. He informed Baker that the club no longer served crabmeat cocktails. Then, before she could place a new order, he turned away.

Baker sat at the table for several minutes, thinking the situation over. She was too angry to let the incident pass, and rising, she walked swiftly to the nearest telephone. Walter Winchell, a widely read newspaper columnist, happened to be dining at the Stork Club the same evening. As Baker passed, he raised his hand in greeting. (She would later claim he ignored her completely.)

Picking up the receiver, Baker told the operator she wished to speak to Walter White, executive secretary of the NAACP. With that simple request, she set into motion a chain of events that would affect her career for the next 15 years. ✑

9

THE RAINBOW TRIBE

By THE NEXT morning—October 17, 1951—Josephine Baker had contacted a deputy commissioner of the New York City Police Department, the executive secretary of the NAACP, and reporters of the *New York Daily News*. To each, she explained what had happened the night before at the Stork Club. The mayor was called, a formal complaint was lodged, and the story hit the papers. Within 72 hours, angry blacks were picketing in front of New York's most famous night spot.

Everything was going just as Baker had hoped. And then she made her one mistake: For some reason, she insisted on dragging Walter Winchell into the matter.

In 1951, Winchell was the most influential newspaper columnist and radio broadcaster in America. More than any other person in the media, he had the power to make and break the careers of actors, politicians, and businessmen. The fashionable Stork Club was Winchell's throne room, and it was there, from Table 50, that he usually wrote his column for the *New York Daily Mirror*. His power was both respected and feared, and those who crossed him in any way were usually sorry.

Baker and Jo Bouillon with nine of their adopted children of different nationalities. When she started this large family, Baker said, "We'll show the world that racial hatred is unnatural, an emotion dreamed up by man; that there is such a thing as a universal family; that it's possible for children of different races to grow up together as brothers."

Baker knew all this when she involved Winchell in her fight against the Stork Club, but she refused to consider the consequences. She saw the matter simply: Winchell, who in the past had spoken out against racial discrimination, had refused to help her in her moment of need. She now considered him a coward and openly said so.

The columnist was furious. At first, he denied having been at the Stork Club at all. Then, rethinking his position, he told his radio listeners he was deeply sorry that Baker had been discriminated against. He added, however, that he was "appalled" she was trying to associate him with the incident in any way.

Many people found themselves taking sides. Prizefighter Sugar Ray Robinson publicly came to Winchell's defense, remembering the times the broadcaster had supported minority rights. The American Newspaper Guild, the NAACP, and Actors Equity all took Baker's side, as did columnist Ed Sullivan, who said on the radio, "I despise Walter Winchell for what he has done to Josephine Baker." Moments later, Sullivan shocked listeners by calling Winchell a "small-time Hitler."

This was going too far, and Winchell exploded. In the past, he had publicly admired Baker as both an entertainer and civil rights spokesperson, but now he was determined to ruin her. In a spirit of near-hysterical revenge, he accused "Josa-phoney Baker" of being not only anti-Semitic but anti-Negro. The charges were ridiculous, of course, but Winchell had a large and loyal following, and many Americans believed whatever he said. The fact that Baker had given up her citizenship did not help, either.

Winchell went on to suggest that Baker was sympathetic to the Communist party and that some of the blacks picketing the Stork Club were themselves Communists. These were very serious charges,

Baker contacted the National Association for the Advancement of Colored People (NAACP) on October 16, 1951, immediately after the Stork Club in New York City refused to serve her because she was black. Her heated response to this discriminatory incident netted some negative publicity that ultimately damaged her chance to become a big star in America.

coming at a time when fear of the Soviet Union's rise as an international power was at a feverish pitch in America. Winchell topped off his accusations by insisting that Baker had spent her war years "making oodles of dough in Paris, wining and dining the Nazis' and Mussolini's bigwig generals."

It was a thoroughly unprofessional attack, one that hurt not only Baker but Winchell himself. Angry letters began pouring into his New York City office, accusing him of being a coward and a bigot. Newspapers and magazines nationwide began criticizing him. The story even reached France, where the Parisian papers referred to it as *l'Affair du Stork*.

The person who was most hurt, however, was Baker. As the weeks passed, she watched helplessly as concert engagements were canceled one by one.

Threatening letters began arriving at her hotel. A film contract she had just signed was suddenly annulled. Plans to write her life story for an American publisher were dropped. Even blacks now kept their distance, quietly changing tables if Baker sat next to them in a restaurant. Few people, it seemed, wanted to be associated with someone Walter Winchell had called a Communist.

The American tour, which had been such a success, now turned sour, and Baker felt deeply disappointed. She continued traveling around the country, promoting civil rights whenever she could, but America no longer wanted to hear what she had to say. At last, Baker realized she was fighting a losing battle, and in the summer of 1952 she returned to her château in the Dordogne Valley.

Construction, she discovered, was progressing smoothly. A restaurant and souvenir shop had been opened, gas pumps had been installed, and small huts were being built for weekend guests. Riding around the estate in a pony cart, Baker was delighted with the improvements.

Even at this early stage, however, the financial stability of Les Milandes depended entirely on Baker's touring. In September, therefore, she was off to Argentina for a concert engagement in Buenos Aires. There, her American problems continued.

In 1952, Juan Perón was the dictator of Argentina. His wife, the beloved Evita, had died of cancer that July, and when Baker arrived, the country was still in mourning. Plans were under way to erect an enormous monument to the memory of Evita, and workers were being asked to contribute their wages to pay for its construction.

Like Baker, Evita Perón was a controversial woman who had risen from a childhood of poverty to a position of great wealth and influence. In 1952, the 33-year-old Evita had been at the height of her popularity. Two million bereaved Argentines had lined the streets of Buenos Aires as her glass-covered coffin passed by.

Baker had been in Argentina only a short time before Juan Perón contacted her. He was deeply grieved by the death of his wife. Evita had been his inspiration, his power—her energy had been largely responsible for his success. Without her, Perón felt lonely and weak. He needed a strong, self-made woman to continue his wife's work, someone who could lead the masses. Someone with a name. Someone like Baker.

Flattered by Perón's compliments, and sincerely believing he was a good and honest leader, Baker agreed to assume some of Evita's duties. At a memorial rally, speaking before a large crowd of working-class people, Baker delivered a stirring speech in which she praised Argentina for being an "enlightened democracy," which it certainly was not. Perón's Argentina was a Fascist state, one which severely limited the rights of its citizens. No one could speak out against Perón without fear of imprisonment.

Baker was very naive, however, when it came to understanding political situations. She rarely troubled herself with learning the facts; almost always, she listened to her heart and acted accordingly. This combination of ignorance and innocence further poisoned her relations with the United States.

Over the next several months, Baker consistently spoke out against America, calling it a "barbarous land living in a false, Nazi-style democracy." Nor did she have any faith in the newly elected president, Dwight D. Eisenhower. "Black people will suffer as they have never suffered," she said. "May God have pity on them." These statements, and others equally harsh, alienated her from the U.S. government and would cause her a great deal of trouble in years to come.

Señora Baker, as she was called, stayed in Argentina for a total of six months, visiting hospitals, meeting with the press, and recommending to the government which charities should receive support. As she understood it, her job was essentially one of goodwill. In reality, it was a mask designed to hide the injustices of Perón's regime.

Gradually, though, even Baker began to see the situation for what it was. She noticed, for instance, that many Argentines were living in terrible poverty, that hospital care was frequently inadequate, and that mentally disturbed patients were treated like animals in the asylums. Evita Perón, she learned, had nearly bankrupted the nation with her extravagant tastes for clothing and jewelry. Baker heard persistent rumors that the army was dissatisfied, that corruption existed at every level of the government, that Juan Perón's secret police used brutal methods to deal with political enemies.

Finally, in the spring of 1953, Baker realized she no longer wanted to represent Juan Perón. Confused and distressed, she returned to France, to the familiar surroundings of Les Milandes. There, she felt compelled to do some serious thinking about her life. Her efforts to end discrimination had been largely unsuccessful, and at the age of 47, she wondered what she could realistically accomplish in the years ahead.

Ever since the end of the war, a dream had been slowly developing in the back of her mind. Now, with Jo Bouillon's help, she wanted to see it come true. It would bring together all of her ideas about equality and what she called the "brotherhood of man."

As Baker saw it, there was no valid reason why all the races could not live together in peace—the world only needed to be shown how. Les Milandes, with its eating and sleeping facilities, large vegetable gardens, church, cemetery, and nearby river, had already

*Les Milandes, Baker's
15th-century estate in the
Dordogne Valley of France. The
estate featured everything from a
farm, a post office, and a bakery
to a restaurant, a theater, and a
wax museum devoted to the
highlights of Josephine's life. At its
height, the establishment attracted
300,000 visitors a year.*

become something of a small city. In her mind's eye,
Baker could easily see it as a global village. (She had
already installed, in fairy-tale fashion, a tiny post
office near the château; its stamps were not recog-
nized by the French postal service, but the post office
made Baker feel as if she were living in her own
private kingdom.)

In this quiet spot, removed from the world's
prejudices, Baker hoped to adopt a large number of
children of different nationalities. By raising them in
an atmosphere of love and equality, she would show
the world that racial harmony was not only possible
but absolutely vital.

As usual, Baker's dream was a costly one, but she
believed in it so passionately she refused to let
anything stand in her way. By 1953, she and Jo had
turned Les Milandes into a lovely resort, with a plush
hotel, a swimming pool, a pleasure garden, paddleboats, a theater, an amusement park, and a special
museum devoted to the highlights of Baker's life. It
was an ideal environment in which to raise children.

In early 1954, after filling several rooms with
baby furniture, Baker set off for Tokyo, Japan. There,
she adopted two baby boys, the first members of what

would come to be known as Josephine Baker's Rainbow Tribe: Akio, a Korean, and Janot, a Japanese.

As a representative of the International League Against Racism and Anti-Semitism, Baker also gave several lectures in Osaka and Tokyo. With the aid of an interpreter, she stressed the importance of worldwide peace. The Japanese listened closely to her ideas. Japan was a defeated nation after World War II, with many of its people suffering from the effects of mass radiation poisoning caused by the atomic bombs dropped on Hiroshima and Nagasaki by U.S. warplanes. The Japanese were eager to avoid at all costs the tragedy of another world war.

Baker enjoyed public speaking, and later that year, she traveled to Scandinavia to give more lectures. While she was in Helsinki, she adopted a two-year-old Finn named Jari, a fat little boy who took great delight in making it as difficult as possible for Baker to pick him up.

Then, in 1955, it was off to Central and South America. One evening in Bogotá, a poor Colombian woman appeared in the lobby of Baker's hotel, carrying a baby wrapped in a dirty shawl. She held the bundle out to Baker, explaining that it was her eighth child and that she could not afford to raise him. Within 24 hours, adoption arrangements had been made, and little Luis joined the Rainbow Tribe.

At this point, Jo became concerned. Financially, he was a cautious, practical man, and he could see that the expenses were starting to get out of hand. He tried to discuss the matter with his wife, but Baker's answer was firm. As long as they could afford governesses, she saw no reason to delay the adoptions. Besides, she felt it was her God-given responsibility to help as many children as she could.

It was not long before the Bouillons had taken in three more infants: Marianne and Jean-Claude, who were French, and Brahim, an Arab. The growing

Tribe attracted a great deal of attention from the press and the public. More than 300,000 tourists flocked to Les Milandes each summer to see for themselves this unconventional experiment in humanity. Still, as Jo's financial records revealed, there never seemed to be quite enough money.

In her attempt to mix children not only of different nationalities but different religions, Baker traveled to Israel, where she tried, unsuccessfully, to adopt a Jewish boy. A new country, Israel was trying to develop its population, and Baker was unable to persuade the government to release an Israeli youngster.

She refused to give up, however, and simply adopted a Jewish child through an organization based in Paris. The boy's name was Moses (Moïse), and Baker would later go to great lengths to provide him with a proper Jewish education. By the time the boy's lessons began, however, little Moses was more interested in sitting by the swimming pool than in studying Hebrew texts. When Baker did nothing to encourage her son's studies, Moses's tutor quit in frustration.

Unfortunately, he was not the first, or last, teacher to angrily walk out the gates of Les Milandes. From the very beginning, Baker stubbornly refused to discipline her children. As an entertainer, she was able to spend only a limited amount of time with the family. It was vital, therefore, that every moment with the children be as enjoyable as possible. Sharp words and spankings had no place at Les Milandes.

Another, more serious, problem was Baker's marriage. Because she was on tour so much of the time, Baker felt removed from the day-to-day problems at the château. She never had to deal with the food shopping or the cleaning of the pool or the checking-in of guests or any of the thousand little details that kept the resort running smoothly. Leaky faucets were

" 'We must go on; we must.' That was Josephine's battle cry" for Les Milandes, according to Jo Bouillon. "She was right, of course. But converting the crumbling château, the pleasure garden and the 120 acres that surrounded them into the setting she dreamed of would be an incredibly costly matter." Baker attempted to earn enough money to cover the renovation costs by working nonstop.

simply not her concern, and over a period of time, she began to regard Jo as little more than the caretaker at Les Milandes. During her brief visits home, she was jealous of the fact that he knew the children better than she did, and his constant lectures about money annoyed her.

Baker realized that her marriage was in trouble, but she did not know how to save it. More than once, she promised to retire, but the cost of running the château and raising eight children was extraordinary. By 1957, the Bouillons were more than 83 million francs in debt. Even if Baker had wanted to quit the stage, it would have been impossible.

For Jo, the breaking point came in early 1957, when Baker brought home a little black boy named Koffi, an orphan from the Ivory Coast. Repeatedly, Jo tried to explain to her the tremendous financial strain she was putting upon the family, but Baker refused to listen. As far as she was concerned, she was working for the good of humankind. This lofty, unrealistic approach led to a series of arguments that eventually shattered the marriage. One afternoon, Baker went so far as to bring the servants together in the hallway, hysterically demanding that they choose between herself and Jo. "If you're on his side, stand over there," she insisted, pointing to the other side of the room.

A separation was clearly in order, and in late 1957 Jo packed his things and moved to Paris, where he resumed his career as an orchestra conductor. He and Baker delayed getting a divorce, though. At heart, neither was anxious to see the marriage end, especially with nine children involved.

With difficulty, Baker took over the management of Les Milandes. Ignoring the 83 million francs she owed, she went ahead and ordered further construction, never even asking what the cost would be. Finances confused and bored her, and she stayed as far away from them as possible.

Instead, Baker devoted her energy to the Rainbow Tribe, taking the children on tour whenever it could be arranged. She particularly enjoyed introducing them to their native lands. In 1958, for instance, five-year-old Jari was able to visit Finland, where Baker was giving a concert in the city of Helsinki. In no time at all, traveling became a happy way of life for the nine youngsters.

In the spring of that year, Jo returned to Les Milandes, determined to rescue his marriage. The reconciliation was bumpy. For one thing, Baker refused to curb her spending habits. On every tour, she bought dozens of new dresses, scarves, blouses, and hats. She also purchased presents for the children, who called her, appropriately, Mama Cadeau (Mother Gift). Ignoring the entertainment budget, she brought in expensive orchestras and ballet troupes, and foolishly, she began buying up all the land around Les Milandes.

Then, to Jo's considerable shock, she adopted 2 more infants, bringing the Tribe to a grand total of 11. The first child, Mara, was a malnourished Venezuelan Indian; the second, Noël, had been abandoned on the streets of Paris. Baker was convinced that God had saved the infants for a reason, and though she knew the adoptions would cause further financial hardship, she could never turn her back on a child in need.

Jo realized then that their differences were irreconcilable. Shortly after Noël's adoption, he packed his things and moved to a small apartment in Paris. The marriage, which had lasted nearly 13 years, was over. •••

10

GREAT DREAMS

———— ❧ ————

In an official ceremony at Les Milandes in August 1961, Baker receives the Cross of the Legion of Honor from General Vallin, commander in chief of the Free French Air Force during World War II. "In your case, peace did not mean rest," he told her. "You found a new role to play on the world stage, that of moral educator. It is the sum total of your contributions as an adopted Frenchwoman that France honors through me today."

LEFT ON HER own, Josephine Baker now embarked on the most turbulent, most stressful period of her life. Lacking Jo Bouillon's business sense, she allowed the debts at the world village to grow astronomical. One by one, merchants began cutting off the steady stream of supplies to Les Milandes. Most of these local tradespeople wanted to see Baker succeed, but, naturally, they could not live on promises and IOUs. There was a time when Baker was so popular she could have walked into nearly any store in Paris, done her shopping, and never have been charged for her purchases. Now, she could not buy a pound of butter without paying cash on the spot.

The only practical solution was for Baker to declare bankruptcy. This she would not do. In her heart, she believed that God was watching out for her. As long as she kept trying, she was certain she would not be forsaken.

In January 1961, it looked like Baker's patience would finally be rewarded. One afternoon, she was contacted by a European director, Ernst Marischka, who was hoping to make a film about the Rainbow Tribe. He was certain the project would be a success, and the money that Baker would receive would be more than enough to save Les Milandes. With one simple signature, all her financial troubles would be solved.

Baker thought the matter over carefully, and finally, after a long, sleepless night, she said no. A movie, she feared, would exploit the children and somehow cheapen what she was trying to do. Above all, she wanted her youngsters to be able to go out into the world and teach other people the racial tolerance they had learned at Les Milandes. She was afraid that a film might change them, alter their outlook and their values. She could not take that chance.

It was an extremely difficult decision for Baker. Little by little, she could see that Les Milandes was slipping away, and the thought agonized her. A few weeks after rejecting the film offer, she sat down and tried to write out her feelings.

"I don't know how or where I'm going," she began. "How will I manage? I have only a few thousand francs left. Everything's going wrong."

Then, in a moment of remarkable insight, Baker added, "But I also realize *how difficult it must be to live with people like me.*"

And yet, despite all her troubles and worries, there were still many happy days at Les Milandes. Life with Josephine Baker was always an adventure, a roller coaster ride full of unexpected surprises. That summer, for instance, she participated in one of the proudest ceremonies of her life, when the French republic named her a Chevalier of the Legion of Honor. The pronouncement was made not only in recognition of her wartime work but for her peacetime effort to educate the world about the injustice of discrimination.

The impressive ceremony took place in August at Les Milandes and was attended by representatives from six nations, including the United States. Baker was deeply moved by the honor. Speaking to the crowd, she commended France as "the only place in the world where I can quietly and surely realize my dream." Afterward, as photographers rushed forward,

Baker takes on the role of animal tamer at a 1961 Paris benefit for elderly artists. Author Jean Cocteau said of her that night, "It's as if the beauty of her heart had rubbed off onto her body."

the Rainbow Tribe hugged Baker around the knees and presented her with bouquets of freshly picked flowers.

That fall, Bosley Crowther, the film critic of the *New York Times*, expressed a desire to write a book about Baker's life. He was not the first person to suggest the idea, nor would he be the last. (As early as the 1930s, there had been talk of turning Baker's life into a play.) Sadly, Crowther's book was never written. In fact, none of the creative projects inspired by La Bakaire ever materialized during her lifetime.

The next few years were agonizing for Baker. She toured constantly, but her income quickly evaporated in poor business decisions and outrageous spending habits. (She found it necessary, for instance, to liven up the barnyard by spelling out the cows' names in electric lights.) By 1963, Les Milandes was nearly $400,000 in debt. The situation was extremely critical, and Baker was forced to sell her jewelry collection to pay the most important bills.

Unwisely, it was at this time that Baker decided to adopt another child: Stellina, the 12th and final

Civil rights leader Martin Luther King, Jr., addresses 250,000 equal rights demonstrators at the Lincoln Memorial in Washington, D.C., on August 28, 1963. When it was her turn to speak, Baker told the crowd, "You are on the eve of a complete victory. You can't go wrong. The world is behind you."

member of the Rainbow Tribe. Stellina was a beautiful but delicate Moroccan baby born in France. For months, little Marianne had been begging for a baby sister, and now she had one. Even Jo Bouillon, who was preparing to move to Buenos Aires, agreed to sign the adoption papers.

As a social experiment, the Rainbow Tribe never achieved great importance. When Baker started her family in 1954, she had hoped to prove to the world that all races could live together harmoniously. If she had limited the adoptions to a reasonable number— say, five or six—the village would almost certainly have flourished. Instead, she adopted twice that many, driving herself to financial ruin. The social value of Baker's experiment was largely ignored by the press, which focused, naturally, on her financial problems. In an age when the issue of civil rights was taking on new importance, it must have sickened Baker to realize that the Rainbow Tribe was no longer newsworthy.

Instead, the fight for equality was being taken up by other, younger activists, few of whom remembered Baker's earlier accomplishments. In America, for instance, definite changes were taking place. More and more blacks were demanding equal justice under the law; segregation was a highly controversial issue; and a 34-year-old Baptist minister named Martin Luther King, Jr., had stepped to the forefront of the civil rights movement. In August 1963, he and other black leaders were planning an enormous march in the nation's capital, a march that would symbolize the importance of black equality.

Baker was determined to participate, but to her shock, the U.S. Department of Immigration stood in her way. Her anti-American statements and Walter Winchell's insistence that she was a Communist had still not been forgotten. Fortunately, the U.S. attorney general, Robert Kennedy, took it upon himself to help her. He convinced his brother, President John

F. Kennedy, to launch an investigation into Baker's political background.

After a thorough inquiry, the Kennedys decided that Baker was not a Communist—or anything else, for that matter. Her beliefs concerning brotherhood were simply too naive to make her an effective member of any political organization. It was obvious, at least to the Kennedys, that she presented no threat to the American government, and instructions were sent to the Department of Immigration to admit Baker without delay.

The March on Washington for Jobs and Freedom took place on August 28, 1963, and was, at the time, the largest civil rights gathering in American history. With 250,000 other equal rights supporters, Baker marched down Pennsylvania Avenue to the Lincoln Memorial, where a large platform had been erected for a rally. It was a hot, sunny day, and the rally, which began at one o'clock, was broadcast over live television. King introduced a variety of speakers, then invited Baker to say a few words. By this time, the heat was intense and the crowd was beginning to grow restless. Baker, wearing her wartime uniform, walked quietly to the microphone and stared out at the sea of people before her.

"I am so happy to be here," she said, her voice choked with emotion.

For the next few minutes, Baker spoke of her difficult childhood in St. Louis, of the equality she had known in France, and the equality that would surely come to the United States. She filled her listeners with hope and dignity and a keen sense of brotherhood. When she finished her speech and turned away from the microphone, the applause was deafening. People stomped their feet and broke into joyous song. Many of them had never heard of Josephine Baker before, but her simple words had convinced them that she was a truly remarkable woman.

Taking her seat, Baker watched as King, the last speaker of the day, stepped to the microphone. With great conviction, he too mesmerized the crowd with a speech that would be remembered as the greatest of his career. "I have a dream," he told his listeners, "that one day this nation will rise up, live out the meaning of its creed: We hold these truths to be self-evident, that all men are created equal."

The effect of the March on Washington was extremely powerful and could be felt all over the country. The following year, in fact, King was awarded the Nobel Peace Prize, and the U.S. Congress passed the Civil Rights Act of 1964, outlawing most forms of racial discrimination. Progress was finally being made.

As Baker boarded the plane to return to France, she was filled with a renewed sense of determination. Now, it seemed more important than ever to save Les Milandes. The problems that awaited her at home, however, were considerable. Not only were the debts enormous, but the situation with the servants was becoming unmanageable. Since Baker could not afford to pay salaries promptly, employees were coming and going at regular intervals. Governesses were almost impossible to keep—they found Baker unpredictable and bossy, and they resented being told how to care for the children. In their bitterness, some of the employees began stealing to get even.

The popularity of Les Milandes was also steadily declining. Interest in the World Village had faded; people preferred to see Baker in Paris, descending the glamorous staircase of the Olympia Theater. The deterioration of the château tormented her terribly. At night, she could not sleep, racked with worry, trying to figure out some way to save the estate. At the age of 57, she knew she could not rely on touring much longer. Somehow, Les Milandes had to become self-sufficient.

Gradually, Baker became convinced that it would be most practical to establish a large school on the property. She even came up with a lofty name for the institution: the International Brotherhood College. The school, which she hoped would attract 500 young adults, would offer a broad variety of courses. The overall emphasis would be on human relations.

Prejudice, Baker believed, was the result of ignorance and distrust. Real freedom, then, could only come about through education. Sadly, people had to learn about equality before they could practice it.

Baker saw her school as quite revolutionary, one that would attract professors and speakers from all over the world. With spacious dormitories and communal eating halls, it would be similar to her global village, only on a larger scale.

The cost of building and maintaining the college would be staggering, but Baker refused to give up the idea. For the next several years, she toured frequently, and in one newspaper interview after another, she explained her financial situation to the public. She was delighted when envelopes containing money began to arrive at Les Milandes. Usually, the envelopes held only small amounts—$5 or $10—but they were a healthy step in the right direction.

Influential friends and celebrities also did what they could to help. Film actress Brigitte Bardot appeared on a French television program that raised nearly $25,000 for Les Milandes. King Hussan II of Morocco, Empress Farah Dibah of Iran, and Yvonne de Gaulle, wife of the president of France, all sent money. A Swiss bank loaned Baker a substantial amount. All this help came just in time: The electricity and water at Les Milandes had been shut off for lack of payment, and Baker's creditors had gone to court to have her possessions sold at auction.

The hard work and constant worry took their toll. On July 25, 1964, Baker suffered a heart attack and was rushed to the Boucicaut Hospital. Even then she could not stop. She had to calculate how much the hospital bill would be and how much work would be required to cover the loss. On October 24, she suffered a second heart attack. Although it was not as serious as the first, it was still a psychological as well as a physical setback.

Plans for the university continued, meanwhile, and in early 1965 Baker contacted an Italian architect, Bruno Fedrigolli, who began drawing designs for the classrooms, dormitories, and offices that would surround the ancient château. Wherever she went, Baker spoke about the college and how it would promote goodwill and understanding among all races.

"We must change the system of education and instruction," she wrote. "Unfortunately, history has shown us that brotherhood must be learned, when it should be natural."

To Baker's surprise, the Cuban dictator Fidel Castro took an interest in her dream. In July 1966, her family was invited to spend a month's vacation in one of Castro's villas. The Cuban holiday was delightful, and each child received a personal gift from "Uncle Fidel" before leaving the island. Castro also promised he would send a special gift to Les Milandes. Naturally, Baker assumed it would be money, enough to save the château and start the college.

She was wrong. When Castro's gift arrived, it was not a check but a large box of Cuban fruit.

King Hussan's generosity proved to be more practical. The Moroccan ruler offered Baker a large piece of land in Marrakech, where she could rebuild her life and begin construction of the International Brotherhood College. The offer was extremely tempting, but in her heart Baker knew she could not turn her back on Les Milandes. Furthermore, she felt it was vital that the college be built in France, which she considered a true democracy.

It was a brave decision, especially because the

creditors were constantly at Baker's side, pressuring her, nagging her. A list had already been drawn up of her household possessions, and Baker knew that any day they might be sold to the highest bidder. Somehow, she managed to raise enough money to avoid each auction, but it was a desperate race against time.

By 1968, not only was Baker's dream crumbling but so was Les Milandes. She could no longer afford to pay gardeners, and weeds began sprouting between the paving stones. Water leaked through the roof, staining the expensive oriental carpets. The paddleboats were faded, their paint peeling off into the water. In February, Baker narrowly avoided another attempt to auction off the château. Her debts at this point totaled a staggering 150 million francs.

When Les Milandes finally collapsed, it happened exactly as Baker feared it would. The creditors could wait no longer, and an auction was scheduled for the spring of 1968. This was an extremely difficult period in Baker's life. Not only was she in dire financial straits, but in April she had heard the news that Martin Luther King, Jr., had been assassinated in Memphis, Tennessee. Another hope for the future of black Americans had been cruelly shattered.

On May 3, the day of the auction, Baker happened to be on tour in Scandinavia. Sitting in her hotel room in Göteborg, Sweden, she nervously watched the clock, waiting for someone to phone her with the bad news. As the minutes ticked by, she tried to jot down her thoughts. "I'm sitting here sick at heart," she wrote. "Will Les Milandes be put up for sale at two o'clock or not? . . . I'm determined to fight this through. . . . The forty-five minutes are up now. The auction has begun."

Three hours later, the phone call came. *"I'm afraid I've got very bad news,"* Baker wrote. *"At four o'clock Les Milandes was sold for 125 million francs."*

Her luck had finally run out. ❧

The end of a dream: Baker sits on the back stoop of Les Milandes in March 1969, after some local toughs hired by the estate's new owner threw her out of the house.

11

ANSWERED PRAYERS

I N JUNE 1968, Josephine Baker's future was an uncertain and troubling thing. She was temporarily out of work, and she would soon be homeless. How could she continue to raise 12 children under those circumstances? Once again, the constant worry took its toll, and on July 4, Baker suffered a minor stroke.

Fortunately, her recovery was swift. Baker was determined to beat her troubles no matter what it took. No sooner had she recovered, however, than Akio, her eldest, had to be rushed to the hospital for an emergency appendectomy. One misfortune seemed to follow another.

A formal notice was sent to Les Milandes informing Baker that she and the children had to be off the property by October 7. The eviction was delayed, however, and the family spent the last remaining months living together in one room, desperately trying to figure out some way to buy back the property. It was a sad, hopeless situation.

The following January, Baker watched helplessly as the furniture was auctioned off, piece by piece. Everything was sold, from the dining room chairs to the cat's food dish. A treasured letter from French president Charles de Gaulle sold for only one franc—the silver frame alone was worth much more than that.

Eager to move into their new home, Baker and her 12 children arrive at the Monaco train station in September 1969. Thanks to Princess Grace of Monaco, who greatly admired Baker's crusade for civil rights, the Monaco Red Cross helped the virtually homeless entertainer obtain a four-bedroom villa near Monte Carlo.

When it came time to leave, the children walked along the banks of the Dordogne, tearfully hugging the trees good-bye. The Rainbow Tribe was then sent to live with a friend in Paris, while Baker stayed behind to fight for their legal rights. She was firmly convinced that she had been swindled, that the property was legally still hers. When it became obvious that the law was no longer on her side, she crawled through a window and barricaded herself in the kitchen. The new owner of Les Milandes had no patience for this sort of behavior, and one morning, he sent over a group of neighborhood toughs to force her out.

The scene that followed was appalling. As the men hauled Baker through the kitchen, she grabbed onto the stove so tightly her fingers had to be pried off. Next, they kicked the back door open and roughly pushed her out, onto the back stoop. She sat there, like a crumpled rag doll, for the next seven hours in the rain. Finally, an ambulance arrived and took her to a nearby hospital, where she was admitted for nervous exhaustion.

After 12 desperate years, the tragedy of Les Milandes was over. Baker had been beaten.

A few weeks later, she returned to Paris, collected the children, and moved to a small, rented apartment on the avenue Mac-Mohon. The sale of the château had done little to ease Baker's financial troubles. There were still many bills to pay and many mouths to feed. At one time, in 1930, Baker had been the wealthiest black woman in the world. Now, she was living in a 2-room apartment with 12 children and 2 dogs. If there was ever a time in her life when she needed help, it was now.

One can easily imagine Baker's surprise, then, when Princess Grace of Monaco offered to lend a hand. In 1969, the princess was one of the most respected women in the world. A beautiful, award-winning actress, she had retired from motion pictures in 1956 to marry Prince Rainier of Monaco. Their lavish wedding was regarded around the world as a fairy tale come true. By coincidence, Princess Grace had been dining at the Stork Club that evening in 1951 when Baker was denied service. She had been deeply upset by the incident and had admired Baker's courage in standing up for her civil rights. Now, reading of Les Milandes's auction, Princess Grace invited Baker to perform at a special benefit that August for the Monaco Red Cross.

Though she would not be paid for her appearance, Baker accepted the invitation. Her performance that summer night created a sensation. For a full 90 minutes, she treated the audience to an unforgettable evening of passionate singing and nimble dancing. When she broke into her famous Charleston, it seemed impossible that this was the same Josephine Baker who, only months earlier, had sat weeping in the rain on her back stoop. The transformation, to put it mildly, was breathtaking. At the end of the show, the crowd threw roses onto the stage while whistling and shouting its approval.

The revue played for an entire week, and word of Baker's triumph quickly spread throughout Europe. To her delight, invitations and contracts began arriving at the hotel where she was staying. Originally, she had planned to return to Paris at the end of August, but now she decided to make her permanent home in the tiny principality of Monaco. With Princess Grace's approval, the Red Cross gave Baker $20,000 as a down payment for a house in nearby Roquebrune, about 3 miles from Monte Carlo. The four-bedroom villa, which she named Maryvonne, clung dramatically to the rocks above the sea.

The Baker clan quickly settled into its new life in Monaco. When Baker was not on tour, she delighted in roaming the picturesque streets, a shopping basket on one arm, several of the children tagging along behind her. In a way, it was the fairy-tale environment she had tried so hard to create for herself at Les Milandes. It was easy to feel like a princess in Monaco.

Little Stellina, the youngest of the Rainbow Tribe, was sent to a local elementary school, where she attended class with Princess Stephanie, Princess Grace's youngest daughter. The other Baker children were growing older and more independent, and to their mother's distress, they no longer needed her as much. Gradually, they had come to resent her continual absences and now remained emotionally distant whenever she returned home from a tour. It was difficult for them to appreciate their mother's hard work, and their indifference hurt her badly. The children were very loyal to each other, however, and Baker was gratified that, in at least one way, her Rainbow experiment had been a success.

The early 1970s were extremely busy for Baker. She continued taking the Tribe on tour, making sure each child was introduced to his or her native country. It was also during this period that the dream of the International Brotherhood College was revived. Marshal Tito, the president of Yugoslavia, had followed the ups and downs of Baker's life, and he knew how much the college meant to her. In a spirit of generosity, he offered her an island off the coast of Yugoslavia where she could live with her family and build her university. He even promised her that the government would install electricity and phone lines, bring in water, and build roads.

Naturally, Baker was tempted to accept the offer. Gradually, however, she realized that, even with Yugoslavian help, the International Brotherhood College would be vastly expensive. She considered selling the villa in Monaco, until she was reminded that the house had not yet been paid for; she could

Baker returns to New York City's Carnegie Hall for a series of concerts in June 1973. Ada "Bricktop" Smith (second from right), who befriended Josephine when she first arrived in Paris nearly half a century earlier, introduced her to the audience at this special four-day engagement.

not sell what she did not own. The Brotherhood College was never built—although, after her initial disappointment, Baker realized it was probably for the best. It would almost certainly have ruined her financially, and she was too old to repeat the tragedy of Les Milandes.

Instead, Baker resumed her international tours. Nearly every concert now was a success, and she felt highly optimistic about the future. In a happy state of mind, she decided to return to America and perform at New York City's prestigious Carnegie Hall. Her old adversary, Walter Winchell, had died the previous year, and her friends felt certain that her return to the States would be a big success.

Baker flew to New York in June 1973, a few days before her 67th birthday. Flyers, meanwhile, were being distributed throughout the city. BLACK LEGEND RETURNS, they announced in large letters. The response was enthusiastic, and when Baker walked onstage opening night, the audience rose to its feet and gave her the warmest, most sincere ovation she had ever received in America. Wild applause echoed throughout the hall, drowning out the orchestra. Tears were filling Baker's eyes before the concert had even begun.

"I didn't think that I would be so well received," she said, deeply moved by the ovation.

Baker's singing voice was no longer the sweet instrument it had once been. That night, in fact, it was particularly hoarse, due to the summer humidity. The audience did not care one bit. They seemed perfectly happy just to be in the presence of the legendary Josephine Baker. As she sang and danced, a single red rose was passed from hand to hand, a delicate symbol of unity and love.

The highlight of the show was a medley of memories from Baker's long and exciting career. She took the audience back to 1925, when she had first arrived in Paris for the show *La Revue Nègre*. There were only a few black people in the city at that time, she explained, and her dark skin had enchanted the Parisians. "They said, 'Isn't it beautiful to be kissed by the sun in that way?'"

At the end of the show, Baker referred to her long struggle against racial discrimination. "Friends and family," she said, "I did take the blows [of life], but I took them with my chin up, in dignity, because I so profoundly love and respect humanity."

The applause that evening was shattering, and the reviews the next day were among the finest of her career. Thrilled with her success, Baker decided to tour the country that fall. In the meantime, however, she flew to Copenhagen for a concert engagement, taking Brahim, Koffi, Noël, and Mara with her.

One afternoon, the four boys sat waiting in the hotel room for Baker to return. After several hours, they decided to call the hospital, where they heard the bad news: She had suffered a heart attack and a stroke. The boys immediately rushed to her bedside, but Baker, barely conscious, did not recognize them. There was nothing the children could do, so they left the hospital and went to the nearest church, where they prayed for their mother's recovery.

Fortunately, Baker was back on her feet within a very short time. It gradually became apparent, however, that the stroke had affected her mind, taking away its former sharpness. Every now and then, she forgot the lyrics to her songs. She confused names and dates. She worried that the public would notice and openly apologized for her mistakes. "I'm too old to play Josephine Baker," she told her friends.

By Christmas, her memory had become so poor that it was almost embarrassing to watch her at times, and this was mentioned in most newspaper reviews. In her heart, Baker knew it would be best to retire quietly, but financially this was impossible. The expenses at the villa were a constant burden. To save money, she began to eat cheap meals and purchase budget clothing for the children. Occasionally, she even asked strangers for money. She was determined to stretch every dollar as far as it could go.

In 1974, the Monaco Red Cross once again invited Baker to perform at its annual fund-raising benefit. This time, the revue not only starred Josephine Baker, it was about her. André Levasseur, the stage designer, wanted the new show to be something special, and *Josephine's Story* seemed the perfect answer. The success or failure of the autobiographical revue would depend largely on Baker's memory, and she accepted the challenge with gusto. As rehearsals got under way, she made it clear that she hoped to take the show to Paris the following spring.

A skillful combination of drama and music, *Josephine's Story* was a hit when it opened in early August. The star's appearance at the beginning of the

"I'm carrying thirty-four years on one shoulder and thirty-five on the other. You add them up!" Baker told the audience at Paris's Bobino Theater on April 9, 1975. Just two months shy of her 69th birthday, Josephine was still so popular that having only her first name appear on advertisements was enough to sell out the engagement weeks in advance.

show was unforgettable: Drawn onstage in a carriage, she stepped out to reveal herself wrapped in 225 yards of fine silk. The effect was stunning, and for the next hour, Baker pulled out all the stops, throwing herself into every song and every dance. The reviews the next morning were glowing. A MILESTONE IN THE HISTORY OF MUSIC HALL, one headline trumpeted.

Sadly, however, the producers could not convince a single theater in Paris to book *Josephine's Story*. The Parisian managers complained that she was a has-been, and to her disappointment, Baker was forced to go on the road again, touring London, Stockholm, Tel Aviv, Johannesburg, and Cape Town. André Levasseur, meanwhile, did his best to convince the Parisian managers to rethink the matter. The show, he told them, could be a sensation if they would only give it a chance.

Finally, after months of meetings and discussions, the Bobino Theater in Paris agreed to stage the revue. Baker was overjoyed and, at the same time, somewhat apprehensive. She sensed that this was her last chance to succeed in Paris; consequently, she pushed herself harder than she ever had before. The rehearsals frequently ran past midnight, but she never complained and was usually the first to arrive at the theater the next morning.

As opening night approached, word spread through Paris that something wonderful was happening in the Bobino. Crowds gathered at the front door, straining to hear the music inside. Onstage, La Bakaire was doing the Charleston, the same dance she had conquered Paris with 50 years earlier. The revue, which had been retitled *Joséphine*, was more than 2 hours long, and the star had to memorize more than 30 musical numbers. It would have been an extraordinary challenge for the youngest of performers. For a 68-year-old woman with a failing memory, it was nothing short of a miracle.

Several performances were given for the public
before the official opening. Each evening, Baker
studied the crowd's reaction, continually tightening
the pace, rearranging songs, dropping entire scenes if
she felt they were slowing down the action. No detail
was too small to be ignored. Baker knew that if the
show was a hit, she could take it on the road and,
within a year's time, earn enough money to finally
retire.

The gala opening on April 8, 1975, was everything Baker hoped it would be. From the moment she
appeared onstage, Paris went wild. It was 1925 all
over again, and the city welcomed her with open
arms.

For the next two hours, Baker held the audience
spellbound as she drove across the stage on a motor-
cycle, danced a furious Charleston, saluted *Shuffle
Along*, paraded down the grand staircase in a variety
of stunning outfits, and, of course, introduced her
favorite animals. She even passed out pieces of
sugarcane; and, sitting in a dusty jeep in her French
air force uniform, she reminisced about the war.

It was as if Baker were trying to squeeze an entire
lifetime into one evening. Yet she succeeded bril-
liantly. The older Parisians wept tears of nostalgia.
The younger Parisians, who knew nothing of Baker,
were amazed. Who was she, they asked, and why had
they never seen her before?

By the time the curtain fell, Baker had recon-
quered the city of her youth. For the next 24 hours,
she was the toast of Paris again: Everyone wanted to
be near her, to touch her, to get her autograph. The
president of France, Valéry Giscard d'Estaing, sent a
telegram congratulating her on her 50-year triumph.
London and New York sent word they wanted to
book the show. Tickets at the Bobino, meanwhile,
were sold out a month in advance. At last, it looked
like Baker's money troubles were over.

Three days after Baker's death on April 12, 1975, a hearse carried her flag-draped coffin through the streets of Paris and brought it to the Church of the Madeleine, where more than 20,000 people waited to say their final good-byes. The nationally televised funeral was attended by ambassadors, celebrities, generals, ministers, and other dignitaries—a spectacular gathering usually reserved for heads of state.

On the morning of Thursday, April 10, Baker slept much later than usual. A friend, Lélia Scotto, who was staying with Baker at the time, could hear light snoring through the bedroom door, so she thought nothing of it. It was not until five o'clock that afternoon that Scotto realized something was wrong. A bit frightened, she rapped on the bedroom door, but there was no answer. Peering in, she discovered Baker stretched out motionless on the bed, newspapers strewn about her. She must have been reading the reviews of her show when, at some point earlier that afternoon, she had slipped into a coma.

An ambulance was immediately summoned, and Baker was rushed to the Salpêtrière Hospital, where she remained in critical condition for the next 36 hours. Word leaked out, and on Friday the hospital was swamped with newspaper reporters and photographers. Princess Grace was in Paris at the time, and she hurried to her friend's bedside, where she prayed fervently for Baker's recovery.

An urgent telegram was sent to Jo Bouillon in Buenos Aires. JOSEPHINE IN SERIOUS CONDITION, it read. He immediately departed for Paris, but sadly, he arrived a few hours too late. Josephine Baker died at 5:00 A.M. on Saturday, April 12, 1975, at the age of 68. The cause of her death was a cerebral hemorrhage. One friend, however, thought differently: "In my opinion, she died of joy."

The funeral, which was held three days later, was an enormous affair. Even though it was a drizzly afternoon, thousands of people crowded the streets to catch a glimpse of the closed coffin as it passed by. Older Parisians, those who remembered Baker well, tossed bouquets of flowers onto the moving hearse. With great pomp, the military fired a 21-gun salute, an honor usually reserved for heads of state.

Inside the Church of the Madeleine, Baker's coffin was draped with the French flag, upon which rested a large cross of red and white roses. Nearby, her war medals were proudly displayed on a satin pillow. Hundreds of candles shimmered warmly as the organist played a selection of Baker's most popular songs, filling the church with rich and extraordinary memories: of triumphs and setbacks, of St. Louis ragtime and the French Resistance, of leopards and monkeys and banana skirts, of dignity and discrimination, and of a noble experiment called the Rainbow Tribe.

It was Josephine Baker's finale . . . a grand exit to a remarkable life. ❧

CHRONOLOGY

1906	Born Josephine McDonald on June 3 in St. Louis, Missouri
ca. 1919	Marries Willie Wells; leaves St. Louis with the Dixie Steppers
1921	Marries Willie Baker
1922	Joins cast of *Shuffle Along*
1924	Stars in *The Chocolate Dandies*
1925	Appears at New York City's Plantation Club; sails for Paris; opens on October 2 in *La Revue Nègre*
1926	Debuts at the Folies-Bergère in Paris
1927	Publishes her first book, *Les Mémoires de Joséphine Baker*; makes her first film, *La Sirène des Tropiques*
1928	Launches her first world tour
1934	Stars in Jacques Offenbach's operetta *La Créole*
1936	Stars in *Ziegfeld Follies* in New York City
1937	Marries Jean Lion; becomes a French citizen
1939	Recruited to work for French military intelligence during World War II
1941	Becomes seriously ill while in Casablanca
1943	Begins touring to entertain Allied troops
1946	Awarded the Medal of the Resistance with Rosette by the French government
1947	Marries Jo Bouillon; purchases Les Milandes in the Dordogne Valley
1949	Opens Les Milandes to the public
1951	Josephine Baker Day is held in Harlem on May 20; the Stork Club incident takes place on October 16
1952	Baker serves as representative of Argentine dictator Juan Perón
1954	Adopts the first of her 12 children of varying nationalities
1959	Her mother, Carrie McDonald, dies on January 12; Baker stars in *Paris Mes Amours* at Paris's Olympia Theater
1961	Named a Chevalier of the Legion of Honor by the French government
1963	Attends the March on Washington on August 28
1964	Suffers a heart attack
1969	Evicted from Les Milandes; moves to Roquebrune, Monaco, with her children
1973	Appears at Carnegie Hall in New York City; suffers another heart attack
1975	Opens in the revue *Joséphine* at the Bobino in Paris on April 8; dies of a cerebral hemorrhage on April 12

FURTHER READING

Baker, Josephine, and Jo Bouillon. *Josephine*. Translated from the French by Mariana Fitzpatrick. New York: Harper & Row, 1977.

Bechet, Sidney. *Treat It Gentle*. New York: Hill & Wang, 1960.

Bogle, Donald. *Brown Sugar: Eighty Years of America's Black Female Superstars*. New York: Harmony Books, 1980.

Bricktop, with James Haskins. *Bricktop*. New York: Atheneum, 1983.

Derval, Paul. *Folies-Bergère*. Translated from the French by Lucienne Hill. New York: Dutton, 1955.

Flanner, Janet. *Paris Was Yesterday, 1925–1939*. New York: Viking Press, 1972.

Hammond, Bryan, comp. *Josephine Baker*. London: Jonathan Cape, 1988.

Haney, Lynn. *Naked at the Feast*. New York: Dodd, Mead, 1981.

Klurfeld, Herman. *Winchell: His Life and Times*. New York: Praeger, 1976.

Long, Richard A. *The Black Tradition in American Dance*. New York: Rizzoli, 1989.

Papich, Stephen. *Remembering Josephine*. Indianapolis: Bobbs-Merrill, 1976.

Rose, Phyllis. *Jazz Cleopatra: Josephine Baker in Her Time*. New York: Doubleday, 1989.

Schroeder, Alan. *Ragtime Tumpie*. With paintings by Bernie Fuchs. Boston: Joy Street Books/Little, Brown, 1989.

Stearns, Marshall, and Jean Stearns. *Jazz Dance: The Story of American Vernacular Dance*. New York: Macmillan, 1968.

Thorpe, Edward. *Black Dance*. New York: Overlook, 1990.

Waters, Ethel, with Charles Samuels. *His Eye Is On the Sparrow*. Garden City, NY: Doubleday, 1951.

INDEX

Page numbers in italics refer to illustrations.

PICTURE CREDITS

———————

ALAN SCHROEDER is a full-time writer and an honors graduate of the University of California, Santa Cruz. His first book, *Ragtime Tumpie* (1989), was a fictionalized account of Josephine Baker's childhood in St. Louis. *Ragtime Tumpie* was selected by several magazines as one of the best children's books of 1989. It was also named a Notable Children's Book of 1989 by the American Library Association. Mr. Schroeder lives in Alameda, California.

NATHAN IRVIN HUGGINS is W.E.B. Du Bois Professor of History and Director of the W.E.B. Du Bois Institute for Afro-American Research at Harvard University. He previously taught at Columbia University. Professor Huggins is the author of numerous books, including *Black Odyssey: The Afro-American Ordeal in Slavery, The Harlem Renaissance,* and *Slave and Citizen: The Life of Frederick Douglass.*